Beauchamps

Dedicated to my grandparents
with affectionate remembrance.

*"Tis but the fate of place
and the rough brake
that virtue must go through"*

- Shakespeare.

BEAUCHAMPS

OR
AFTER GRANDPAPA MET GRANDMAMA...

A Country Story
by
W. Eileen Davies

K.A.F. BREWIN BOOKS

First published in November 1988 by
K.A.F. Brewin Books, Studley, Warwickshire B80 7LG

© W. Eileen Davies 1988
All rights reserved
ISBN 00 947731 44 X

Made and printed in Great Britain
by Supaprint (Redditch) Limited.

PREFACE

This true story is about a family who occupied a Worcestershire farm, a building which has recently been attracting Midland country news because of its antiquity.

It tells of the first five years of that occupation which, from 1880, passing from father to son, and son to son, lasted in all for a hundred and three years.

None of the characters concerned in the narrative are still living, but as author, I have written down my personal interpretation of facts which have been collected from various sources.

Apart from my own affection for the farm and for the occupants of those first five years (my mother having been born there) my further interest was aroused on reading a hand-written journal by Edgar Quinney, her elder brother. Before he died in 1961 he wrote about his memories of the time he lived at Seechem.

The story in this book is based first of all upon that journal.

Other sources are taken from the recollection of members of the Quinney family still living and, where those have needed more details, old newspapers of the time, discovered at the offices of the Redditch Indicator and publishing offices in Bromsgrove, were made readily available.

To confirm the current agricultural background of those years I was particularly indebted to R.C. Gaut's "A History of Worcestershire Agriculture and Rural Development"; also to help given by both Redditch and Bromsgrove Libraries. The public events that interested and affected the personalities in the tale were verified by a "Dictionary of Dates". Old newspapers again, gave 'on the spot' details of Stratford Mop, the hiring of labourers, the Penny Readings, the contemporary conditions of the Workhouse and the murder of the policeman.

An appendix gives details, recently revealed by Stephen Price and Nicholas Molyneaux, two archaeologists to whom we owe thanks, of a history going back to mediaeval times, coming forward to the era when this story begins. As it will be seen, no-one in the narrative knew that history, though the house itself gave clues.

NOTES

Places:

Towns, villages and countryside are given their own names. The farm, which has a personality of its own, is given a pseudonym: "Beauchamps" meaning "Beautiful Fileds" - a true description of the farm's surroundings, and a name close to the real one in sound - Seechem.

The farm "Shortbridge", belonging to the grandparents of the story, stood in reality on the site where now stands the present Longbridge Austin Motor Works.

People

Although all the characters of the story are real and what happens is true, all is seen through the perspective of the author's affectionate regard and is therefore her interpretation of past events. It is for this reason that all but three are given pseudonyms.

The family pseudonym "Yeoman" is self-explanatory and symbolic.

The landlord of "Beauchamps" under his real name became three times Lord Mayor of Birmingham.

The odd-boy at farm is given his real name - John Brown (or Jack) - as real as the others he gained by his exploits.

Johnny Always Drunk and Alvechurch Charlie are not pseudonyms.

Illustrations

"Beauchamps" is drawn from an 80 to 90 year old water colour sketch. It shows that none of the beams on the outside of the house has as yet been uncovered.

Quotation

on title page is from Henry VIII Act 1 Scene 2 William Shakespeare.

CONTENTS

PREFACE AND NOTES .... v & vi

CHAPTER

		Page
1	Departure	1
2	Turning Eastward	3
3	Incident on the Way	6
4	At the Smithy	9
5	Arrival	12
6	The Kitchen Oven	14
7	"Up the Hill"	17
8	"There was a Lovely Lady"	20
9	The Visitors	23
10	The House	28
11	The Farm	31
12	Misfortunes	35
13	Spenser's Arrival	39
14	Comings and Goings	44
15	Mops	48
16	"The Spike" 1882	52
17	The New-comers	55
18	Manures	60
19	Jack goes Hunting	65
20	A Shocking Crime	71
21	Justice is Seen to be Done	76

APPENDIX

"Beauchamps is based on Seechem Manor seen here at the turn of the century. The author's mother is on the right of the group of three.

"Victoria" and "John Yeoman" are based on Caroline and George Quinney seen in this photograph in old age as the author remembers them.

Chapter 1

DEPARTURE

John Yeoman locked the door of Cotewood Farm for the last time. It was Lady Day, March, 1880.

Standing there on the step, he stopped, and sent a careful look around him.

Then, quickly dropping the heavy key into his pocket, he turned, reached into the recess of the porch with its green wooden shelter, picked up the shot gun and a sack, and ran with them down the path to the farmyard.

He had crossed the little green iron bridge that spanned the miniature moat running square round the boundary of the garden when he saw Old Harry. Harry Dock was his wagoner and general labourer on the farm and he was closing the back of the wagon which held twelve sheep, nudging each other fretfully.

For a moment John stopped again, looked round the farmyard with its neat array of green arched doors, all closed.

'Stables bolted and coach house door securely locked, Harry?' he called.

'Aye, maister, they be,' came the answer.

'Follow us along the road to Bromsgrove. If you lose sight of us we'll be waiting at the provision shop at the bottom of the High Street.'

He ran on toward the high trap where his wife, Victoria, was sitting on the hard front seat, staring blankly at the farmyard gate. It stood wide open to the road ready for their departure, and the roan mare, harnessed to the trap, was standing patiently waiting, giving an occasional shake of her head and a pull at the reins.

On the back seat sat Old Sarah, Harry Dock's wife and house servant to the Yeomans. Her eyes were watering with the cold wind as she watched her husband climb with stiffening joints into the wagon with the sheep. Their eyes met across the open, spacious yard. They knew one another's thoughts. They knew what each was thinking now as their eyes turned to look at the coach house where, for two years they had enjoyed their relatively comfortable quarters.

'There'll be none of that where we're a-going. But wagoner and washerwoman us'll have to take what comes our way and make the best on it, if us dunna want to end up in the workus.' They had said this to each other this last morning.

John, reaching the trap, thrust the sack into Sarah's hands and said, 'Push this under the seat out of sight, Sarah.'

Her voluminous skirt already covered a variety of portmanteaus, carpet bags, wicker baskets full of all the things pushed in at the last moment of packing, and the expression on her face said so as she held the sack at arms length in protest.

Victoria had turned at the sound of her husband's voice. She spoke quietly. She knew what the sack held.

'Give me the sack - and the gun. I'll push them under from the front.'

She took the sack from Sarah, stooped and worked it past the wicker cradle on the floor, where their nine month old son lay sleeping, unaware of the upheaval taking place around him. A brace of pheasants and a couple of dead hares lay in the sack that now kept him company. Victoria had seen her husband come in with them first thing that morning.

It was still illegal to shoot game on tenanted land. She took the gun and manoeuvred it into what space there was left, then turned and mechanically retrieved the reins from the floor where she had dropped them.

John Yeoman flung himself into the driving seat, took the reins from his wife's hands and shook them furiously. The roan mare, startled by the unusual action, jerked forward sharply, and, almost thrown off their balance, Victoria and Sarah clung to the seat rails.

As they passed out of the gateway on to the road, both women gave a last quick glance at the place they had both loved and were leaving.

Victoria recalled that day, two years ago when, as a nineteen year old bride as small as the Queen whose name she bore, she had been carried, a feather-weight, over the threshold by her tall, dark-bearded husband. The tears flowed down her cheeks now, and she could hardly endure to look at the lichened seat of weathered oak encircling the base of the old chestnut tree on the front lawn.

On the few sunny days there had been in the starved and flooded first years of their marriage they had both found their way out there to sit, like bleached plants deprived of light, Victoria sewing small garments for their first child, her husband working at the little green iron table on his figures. It was those figures which so soon changed his beard-fringed face from confidence to care.

The trap flew past the moat now hidden from sight behind the low brick wall separating the garden from the road, and only Old Sarah looked at the yew tree on which she had spent any leisure hours she had, clipping it into the shape she desired.

Behind them Old Harry was passing out of the farmyard and, as he leaned from the wagon to close the gate, he looked once more at the empty dove cote and pigeon house. His eyes moved upwards to the green bell tower over the coach house roof to see if any stray white or grey bird remained there. But all was now tenantless and forsaken.

Slowly, lumberingly he drove the farm wagon into the road, following his master through the cold dry air of a March day to the new home ten miles away on the eastern border of Worcestershire.

Chapter 2

TURNING EASTWARD

The turnpike road was in a good state of repair, which was just as well for the roan mare was galloping along it in fine fettle.

Victoria and Old Sarah were both clinging fast to the seat rail. When each had regained their balance after the first lurch forward by the pony and trap, Victoria had reached down to steady the cradle between her feet, quietening the child in his startled awakening, and Sarah had taken the basked of bantams from the floor to give them greater security on her capacious lap; then the two women had anchored themselves securely in the swaying vehicle.

They passed the empty meadows on left and right. Empty, that is, of sheep, and as far as John Yeoman was concerned no other stock counted. For the last six months he had been obsessed with these dead, dying and ailing animals. It was the stench of death in his nostrils and in his memory that now caused his hands to shake the reins so violently, urging the horse forward, away, away.

Victoria knew what he felt for she had herself walked around the autumn fields and had seen the sheep lying stiff and emaciated in death, their beautiful eyes plucked out by the crows.

She remembered his conviction, expressed when they first came to the farm, that the sheep would bring them a comfortable livelihood in spite of the preceding years of aggravated depression in farming. John had said optimistically, 'One year balances up with another and if the last four have been bad, the next four will be good, you mark my word. Sheep have always been and still are the bed-rock of farming.'

It had not been so. The sheep which he had relied had brought him ruin. He was down to rock-bottom only two years later, and his wife knew that the fault lay neither in him nor with the animals but with that fickle jade whom no man had yet been able to tame — The Weather.

Had the weather given them the ordinary, everyday, changeable English climate Yeoman's judgement might have been right. It had not been three or four consecutive bad seasons but six, the last two being the worst within any living farmer's memory, and the result had been liver fluke, a sheep scourge which had been the cause of death for flock upon flock across the length and breadth of the land.

Victoria turned in her seat to look at her husband as he muttered one word again and again, 'Snails! Snails! Snails!' Startled, she asked, 'Why are you so upset over so small a creature?'

For a moment he looked at her as though he did not see her. Then he answered despairingly, I can't explain, Vic. But what I do know is that the years of wet weather have brought snails, battalions of 'em, and when they come fluke comes with 'em. It's been known before.'

The reins slackened in his hands as they approached the market town of Bromsgrove and the mare began to slow down. When they drove into the High Street he drew up at the general stores and sat waiting while Victoria helped the old servant down the step to the ground, then from under the seat the two women disentangled from all the other objects packed there a basket each, and with the large carpet bag between them they set off to buy in a stock of food to last until the next market day.

John Yeoman sat in a brown study seeing no one. He dipped his hand into the pocket of his coat and taking out the door key he had dropped there, he studied it as though it held the secret of his failure and the cure for the future.

He thought of the old farming maxim: "Rent off the sheep to pay the landlord. Rent off the corn to pay the labourer. Rent off the cattle to pay yourself." His father had made it work. He had failed.

When the two women returned and loaded up the trap with their purchases the farmer gave a signal to the horse and they proceeded up the main street looking neither to right nor left, not wishing to see any known face. Reaching the land agent's office at the top end of the town, Yeoman dropped down, leaving the reins in his wife's hands.

The agent was a short stocky man with side-whiskers sprouting sandily from bucolic cheeks and his small blue eyes watered as the cold draught blew in with John's entrance. He said, 'Good morning to ye, Mr. Yeoman, dry day for a change.'

The farmer made no answer, took out the keys of Cotewood with the exact amount of money due for the last rent and threw them on the table. To him the agent represented an absent landlord, who, John believed, had plenty of money, but little understanding of the land and its problems.

As he waited for the receipts to be made out the young farmer thought bitterly of the day when he had driven over to the landlord's well-equippped mansion. In his mind's eye he saw again the purple curtained room where he had sat uncomfortably forward on a grey velvet settee and he had pleaded with the man. He, John Yeoman, proud, independent and hard-working, had debased himself by begging for more time to put the farm back on its feet.

He had put before the landlord a full picture of the troubles of the year - of the two years, in fact, 'Sir, the storms flattened the crops, and on the lower ground carried the wheat away. Haymaking went on until October, an unheard of time to finish. Six weeks late with the harvest and the wheat yielded soft unripened grain; the flour, after being ground at the mill had to be dried on sheets before it could be baked.'

With the landowner listening Yeoman could see by the expression on the man's face that the present state of agriculture meant for the proprietor only a loss of revenue and an increasing embarrassment. The farmer tried another argument.

'Sir, the British Government itself is encouraging councils to reduce rates, and landlords to do the same with rents.' It had all been to no purpose. His words had no effect. He could see that this landlord was not inclined to agree with the Government. He heard the final judgment given.

'Yeoman, if you are unable to make the land pay, it is time your tenancy ended. Next Quarter Day must see you out of Cotewood.'

It was his agent who now was pushing the papers across the table towards the farmer and saying, 'I understand, sir you negotiated last autumn for the tenancy of a farm at Rowney Green, Alvechurch. I happen to know that farmstead has been empty all winter, but the land is in good heart, sir. Thank ye, sir, and good luck to ye in your new home.'

He received no reply. For a minute or two John Yeoman stood there as if deaf. He was seeing before him, not the agent, but the landlord himself.

He picked up the papers and strode from the room without a word.

It was Lady Day, March 1880, one of the two days when, in the year, tenancies began or ended — it was both for John Yeoman. This Worcestershire farmer was leaving a home under one landlord, and moving to a farmstead under another.

Chapter 3

INCIDENT ON THE WAY

The narrow road was crossed here and there by natural springs emerging from the red sandstone through which the lane had been cut and the mare splashed her way through Burcot, a small village on the ancient east-west route, turning east again into Frog Lane, so named because of its extreme wetness and the creatures that abounded there.

Approaching a bridge under a long railway incline John Yeoman turned to his wife and asked, 'You did go to the station last week to make sure there are no trains at this time of the day?'

'Yes, I did. There were none on the time-table.'

'I can hear something that sounds like one,' remarked John apprehensively.

Victoria listened. 'It must be an extra. Shall we turn round and go back a little till it's passed over the bridge?'

There was no time to do this however, for Harry Dock, having made up time during his master's delay in the town, was at that moment bringing up the rear with the wagon load of sheep and the lane was too narrow for either to pass the other at this point.

The locomotive, a long crawling goods train, was making its slow way down the Barnt Green to Bromsgrove incline towards the bridge where they were standing in the road below the track. The mare heard it and stopped dead, her ears well forward, her head up and her body quivering. No amount of coaxing or shouting from John produced any effect on her, she would not take a step nearer the bridge under which she must pass and over which the train was now rumbling.

All would have been well, and they would simply have waited there until the monster had passed out of the animal's sight and hearing but, as the guard's van at the rear passed over the bridge, the engine at the front let out a loud screeching whistle as it approached the distant station.

This was too much for the mare. She half-reared with fright, then bolted forward, followed by the startled wagon horse behind them, and the farmer's wife, almost thrown out of her seat, once more grabbed the seat rail with one hand and the cradle with the other, thankful that she had strapped the child in, since she had no opportunity to pick him up.

Sarah, at the back, in making the same quick snatch at the rail, lost her grip on the bantam basket and, as she was thrown violently first backward, then forward, the basket of birds was catapulted out on to the grassy bank at the side of the road, which was fortunate for them or they would have been tramped under foot by the pursuing wagon horse.

Harry Dock and John Yeoman were both holding on to the reins of their two vehicles unable to do anything but try and gain control over the runaway horses. The mare, with her lighter load, seeing nothing but a clear road ahead, passed under the bridge without hesitancy and, racing along round blind corners regardless of the wildly swaying vehicle to which she was harnessed, put a good distance between the trap and the wagon.

As they approached the Half-way Oak, a large tree overhanging the lane half-way between the town they had left and the village toward which they were travelling, the gallop changed down to a canter and it was not long before the canter became a subdued trotting.

Meanwhile the old wagoner had been delayed. The fright which had driven the mare under and past the bridge had produced the opposite effect on the wagon horse, for the sudden shadow beneath the arch stopped the heavier animal in his forward charge and he pulled up in uncertain apprehension.

This gave Harry Dock the advantage he needed. He had seen the bantam basket fly out of the trap, but had not been able to stop in time to pick it up. Now he climbed down, quietened the horse with soothing words, led him to a stile in the hedge and, tethering him there, he went back to collect the bantams. For the sheep, having been thrown about in the lurching wagon, this must have proved a welcome break, and it was only because they had been tightly packed together that no harm had come to them.

Some distance ahead the mare was making her way more and more slowly uphill and at the top of the ridge she came to a halt, giving the forward party a chance to draw in to the side of the lane where the mare could recover her wind, and the rest could examine the situation in the trap.

Sarah had almost been thrown out with the bantams. Her feet had slipped from the crate of eggs as she twisted herself round to reach for the rail, and the crate, freed from its mooring, had slid first forward and then backward in company with all the other articles packed under the seat, finally ending in collision with the cradle where a shower of eggs broke over the child in a shining stream of albumen and yolks.

Victoria took her son from the wicker cot to calm and reassure him, and as she sat him upon her lap the broken eggshells that bespattered his small person transferred themselves to her own plum-coloured worsted wool coat, glued there by the albumen.

She looked up at her husband to find that the grimness of his face had relaxed as he gazed down at the sight his wife and child presented, and glad that he was less tense and tragic, thankful that they had all survived the rough ride without injury, she said calmly, 'Do we look like scrambled eggs?' The corner of her mouth lifted and, as he looked at the two small figures, so trim when they had set out, now so egg-stained, the young farmer's lips curved in a reluctant smile. He gazed at the quiet face of his wife framed in the dark ringlets. Her hat, encircled with artificial pansies, had fallen sideways over the curls. Nothing, he thought, nothing ever seems to ruffle you, and he grew calm as she returned his long scrutiny with a twinkle in her hazel eyes.

Sarah suddenly cried out from behind them, 'Lookyer! Lookyer! That view!' They turned to look back the way they hd come and toward the south-west, beyond the undulating countryside, they could see the long hazy outline of the Malvern Hills.

They waited there for Harry to join them and as he drew level he called out, 'Oi've got them bantams all right, missus. But maister, Patch's cast a shoe. There be a forge in Alvechurch village, be I to stop and get 'un shod agin?'

John said one word, 'Aye', but as he turned to resume the journey he called back, 'Better get a credit note and tell the farrier I'll pay him next time I'm down in the village.'

Victoria tugged at his coat and said, 'Lookyer, look once more at that view, John. We shan't see it again once we pass over the ridge.' As they took one more last look, she said, 'And we too, my lad, will rise up like those hills out of the mist.' Her husband made no reply, but Sarah said, 'Oh, ah, missus, God willin', an' so ye will. God bless the pair on ye, an' the little child too.'

They made their way down the hill into the village, crossed the square, passed the timber and brick houses and pulled up at the mill in the hollow, where the farmer bought and loaded on a sack of flour.

Then, leaving Old Harry in the village making his way to the forge, they continued about two miles eastward before turning off half-way up the long winding slope of the Weatheroak Hill into the old Roman trackway to the south and, making their way along between its leafless hedges, they came at last to the drive leading to Beauchamps, their new home.

Chapter 4

AT THE SMITHY

Back in the village Harry Dock tethered Patch to the iron ring outside the smithy then, ungearing and lowering the shafts, he left the wagonful of sheep in front of the wide doors and went in to find the farrier.

George Goster was standing before the furnace in the workshop, while a young lad of about thirteen or fourteen years of age, at work on the bellows, was blowing the coal to a red-hot heat into which a thin rod of iron was thrust and held steady by the blacksmith's grip on the tongs.

Shirt sleeves rolled back, in the light of the fire the thin ripple of the lad's muscles contrasted with the greater play of the man's and both gleamed wet with perspiration. Shirts open to the waist showed the boy's skin as smooth as a girl's, the smith's covered with hair that glistened damply in the glowing flames.

The place was faintly illuminated by light glimmering through windows so grimy that it seemed that full daylight was never intended to penetrate the firelit glow of the interior, and by the time Harry Dock's eyes had accustomed themselves to the scene the rod was heated and removed to the anvil where, with rhythmic ringing blows of the hammer, the smith wrought the iron into a sharpened spike.

The wagoner watched, waiting until the poker end was fashioned, then he called, 'Blacksmith! Nice work that. Can ye turn shoesmith to me hoss wot's lost one of his irons?'

'Ah, I can, man,' was the answer. All his "I's", like Harry's were pronounced "Oi" and with no "H's" in his vocabulary his accent was a mixture between the wagoner's broad Worcestershire and the Brummagem dialect. 'Where is he?'

'Outside on the ring. Shall I bring un in?'

'Ah, do that, man Will ye join me in a pint o' bitter? Me lad'll slip up to "The Ammer an' Anvil" for it. I get a right thirst on me in this 'ere 'eat.'

The smith turned to the lad and said, 'Take the brass off the shelf there, Simon.' The youth picked up the money from the ledge and, drawing his shirt together against the outside temperature, disappeared.

'Wot's ye name then, smith?' Harry enquired. The two men exchanged names and the wagoner had related the course of events during which Patch had lost his shoe before Simon returned with the beer.

'Took a long time this morning, din't ye?' questioned the smith.

'Ad to get extra,' explained the boy. ''Ad to wait for it.'

'Fetch the nag in then lad, and be nippy about it.' Turning to Harry he asked, 'Coming this way for keeps then?' He drank his ale off in deep draughts, then turned to examine Patch's shoeless hoof.

The wagoner sipped his ale in small doses and kept a beady eye on Goster's methods. Farriers varied from smithy to smithy and, since a new shoesmith would be a necessity, he wished to give his master a fair account of the way this one would serve.

He watched the paring and cleaning of the sole, the fitting of the shoe as it was thrust smoking hot on the hoof rim, and he made his own judgement as to whether the iron was right for Patch, not too heavy, not too light, how many nails used and what kind of hold given them; and without once taking his eyes off the job in hand, Harry answered the smith's questions.

'I'm going with me maister to Beauchamps, Ye'll know the place I reckon.'

'Oh ah. The old farmer from there ent bin down for a shoeing for a long time. I heard in the vilage as he sold up his furniture last Martinmas and moved out. He was getting on in years ye know, and I heard tell as how he's moved in with his son down Evesham way. So it's ye master wot's taking his place then?'

'Ah, that's about it,' replied Harry. 'And he's just about starting from scratch, as they say fer he's going there with next to nothing but this 'ere hoss an them ship outside wot ent worth keeping alive.' (The clipping of the 'e' in 'sheep' was a general habit among the farming community in Worcestershire. John always kept to it himself.)

'Wot's got 'em then?'

'Ship fluke, like many another.'

'Ah, there be few farmers around these parts with ship that ben't touched with that complaint.'

'If ye'd bin with me maister this last twelve months ye'd a' knowed,' Harry replied. 'A sin and a shame it were to see him.' He listened to the rhythmic sound of the blacksmith's hammer "Ten Pound Ten" — "Ten Pound Ten", then he went on with his story of woe:

'He lost all his flock but these uns in the wagon outside, and drat me if them'll all be alive by the time we reach the new place. I tell ye I seen him, me maister, with me own two eyes, putting his head again' the barn door when he thought not a body was looking, and there he were a-sobbing like a chile.' He stopped a moment, remembering. Then he went on.

'And I'll say this fer un, no matter wot trouble he were in, he paid me wages. I be a-wearing out and glad to get me food, and not being as hearty as I were I'm a bit cheaper to hire than a young un, or I dessay me maister woudna be able to keep me missus and me at all. Things any better this way?'

'About as bad as where you come from, man,' answered Goster. 'We had winter all summer here, same as you. Oh, ah, the farmers wot bring their 'osses 'ere, their flocks have disappeared in a belching cloud of evil-smelling smoke, as the devil said of his own. I did hear tell of one landowner down Henley way as bought out all the farmers in the district. Took up six of the farms and turned them into one. Then all the farmers had to turn shepherds and stockmen to save their families from starvation.'

'Garn?' ejaculated the wagoner. 'Ye don't say! Tellin' a feller a thing like that when he's just arriving! It fair makes ye sweat to think of it, with me maister a-coming this way to start afresh like, and him with a wife and chile on his hands and all.'

'Well he ent got six brats with empty bellies to fill like some folks as I knows of!' was the blacksmith's lugubrious reply.

'You're a sounding like a fayther blackbird!' remarked Harry. 'Hey! You ent got six have ye?'

The farrier was finishing the nailing and did not hear the question; but as he put the horse's hoof down reshod he heard the wagoner say, 'Eh, well, there's landlords and landlords, that's a fact. The last un me maister had didn't give 'im much help to my mind. So here's hoping the next uns a better un.' Harry Dock drank off the remainder of his beer and put the tankard down on the window ledge.

'Oh, ah, there's landlords and landlords, I'll give ye,' agreed the smith, collecting the tools.

'Ah,' Harry added, 'and there's farmers and farmers, and farriers and farriers, and I can see you're a good un. Now me maister he said to give the account to me and when he next comes this way he'll pay ye. And don't ye go giving him any black pictures like ye just bin giving me, me lad!'

'Eh! but this shoeing on credit, now. All the farmers are doing it — and wot about me?'

'Ye can take it from me ye'll not be the loser for it. Me maister won't see me in want, and he won't let you down neither. He ben't that sort of man.'

Chapter 5

ARRIVAL

Victoria dropped lightly down from the trap and opened the gate for her husband to drive through. Then, jolting and swaying up the rutted drive, they came to a second gate where the tall elms stood like sentinels on either side and from which at the approach of the travellers, rooks flew up with raucous cries.

The wheels of the trap slushed wetly through the March mud as they passed the large brick-built barn and caught a glimpse of their new home. John Yeoman looked down at his wife. Taking her hand in one of his he drove toward the gabled house which seemed to peer at them from between the bare branches of the garden trees. The mare approaching a division of the track, became aware of the slackness of the reins and slowed down to a snail's pace as she moved through the unfamiliar surroundings.

In front of them, set in the garden hedge, a small, white-painted iron gate closed on the path leading down to the front door. The young Yeomans afterwards admitted to one another that they had half expected to see a monk emerge from beneath the serene old arched porch and make his way across the lawn to the beehive that was just visible between the bushes. There was something monastic about the atmosphere of the place, and again they received the impression that the house was watching their approach as though possessed of a personality of its own as living and aware as they were themselves.

John Yeoman twitched the reins and the mare moved toward the farmyard pricking her ears inquisitively as they passed a tethered horse at the entrance where the farm gate stood open for their arrival.

Reaching the centre of the yard there was a 'Whoa now, Daisy!' and the mare obediently stood still while Sarah began her laborious descent from the trap.

Gazing around them the farmer and his wife could see that they were in the centre of a square of buildings of which the house itself formed the northern line. A long cowhouse and the farm gate through which they had just entered marked the eastern boundary. Stables, saddle room, a low brick wall against the orchard and a long gate made up the southern rim, while along the western side were the pigsties, another stable and stone steps leading up to a granary, topped by a weather cock turning in the wind.

John sighed. It was impossible not to give way to a momentary return of depression as he became aware of the repairs necessary on walls and roofs. He dropped down from the trap, gave Daisy her bag of bait, then stood there, looking around, frowning.

His wife, sensing his change of mood, went into action. She stepped down from the trap, reached for the basket of retrieved bantams, handed them to Sarah and, lifting her son from the cradle, she walked with him to the back door into the house.

Entering the kitchen she found that, in the centre of the confusion with articles of furniture here, there and everywhere, a space had been cleared for the deal table freshly scrubbed to a shining whiteness.

From end to end it was spread with plates of good wholesome food. There was bacon from the flitch, cream cheese, butter from the churn, eggs from warm nests and bread baked in the oven at Shortbridge, the home of John's father and mother.

Amelia and Joseph Yeoman, the senior parents of the large Yeoman family, had travelled the six miles between farms to superintend the arrival of the household goods from Cotewood.

'Come in, children, and eat?' Amelia called to them in that voice of hers which, while deepening with encroaching age, yet retained that pleasant homely quality that made all her five sons and their families feel welcome wherever it was heard.

'Father', she added comfortingly, 'shall go out and unharness Daisy after the meal is over. Sarah, leave those bantams outside and come and sit down. Father, find some chairs. And Edmund, me dear, come to your Granmer while yer mother and father have a bite to eat.'

The travellers sank thankfully down on seats disentangled from the surrounding jumble and allowed the parents to welcome them to a house that was not yet a home.

Then, hunger abated, the company separated, Joseph Yeoman making for the yard to deal with the trap and its contents, and to ascertain that both horses had sufficient bait to keep them content.

Edmund was left with a delighted Sarah, for whom nursing the child was always a pleasure and an honour. He was a placid babe and Sarah's simple mind harboured the belief that he was too good for this world and would shortly be removed from their midst to take place among the shining throngs of angels that inhabited the old woman's vista of heaven.

John Yeoman and his wife, accompanied by Amelia, began the tour of the house to decide where the furniture was to go. Then, as they were about to start on the work, Old Harry came into the yard, the sickly sheep had to be attended to and folded for the night, the wagon horse unharnessed and stabled.

It was very late when Joseph and Amelia prepared to leave for home. Before climbing into the trap beside his wife, Joseph turned to his son and said, 'Lookye lad, you can't go about in a wagon. We've got two hosses and two traps. You can keep Daisy and the trap you came in, you can borrow another farm hoss and pay me for 'em when ye've got the brass to do it with!' Then, not waiting for thanks which would have embarrassed him, he jumped up beside his wife and drove away at speed.

Chapter 6

THE KITCHEN OVEN

The whole household arose the next morning with the sun. Old Sarah came stumping down the back stairs from the room above the kitchen where she and Old Harry had settled in. She got the fire going in the great black kitchen range (which she viewed with deep distaste, since it had rusted over during the winter months) and cut fat slices off the flitch of bacon John had hung from a beam in the ceiling.

The old servant fried large rounds of home-baked bread in the sizzling fat and, as the two men pulled on their boots ready for an immediate exit after the meal, the room was filled with that perfect aroma which can only be produced from the home-cured bacon of an age that has gone.

Tea brewed, Sarah poured out large mugs full of the golden liquid which the men drank heavily sweetened but milkless, not because there was as yet no cow to give them milk, but because they liked it that way.

The last ritual of the meal was to dunk toast, browned on the end of a toasting fork in front of the red-hot embers into the steaming beverage. The taste was of such effect that John Yeoman's features had that look of contentment which no other item of culinary excellence ever succeeded in creating there. His farming world might fall about his ears but if there were hot toast to be dunked in sweet tea there was still a luxury left to enjoy.

When the two men had gone out to see to the sheep and investigate the farmlands, Sarah did what she had set her mind on from the moment she had arrived. She got down on her knees and attacked the rust on the range, and having worked it to a certain smoothness she black-leaded it with great gusto. 'Eh! It'll be better when I've done it a few times,' she said with satisfaction.

She filled up the heavy iron pot with soft water from the pump at the sink, and the big black kettle with spring water from the pump outside the back door, then went off to see what could be done with the straightening still necessary throughout the house.

Victoria brought in Edmund and set him in his high wicker chair. He had slept soundly through the night, unaffected by what might have been the unsettling experience of being put to bed in a strange place. Strapped in he sat there viewing his changed world with equanimity and a contented gurgle while his mother turned her attention to the preparation of food.

In the dairy she found that her mother-in-law, knowing the young wife would be hard pressed on that first day after the move, had left pigs' trotters ready cooked, potatoes peeled ready for boiling and a baked treacle tart all lined up on the cold slate tram. 'Thanks, mother,' she murmured under her breath and went on to the next chore.

Opening the baking oven she took hot embers from the fire and shovelled them on to the bricks that lined the base, closing the door for the interior to become heated. 'Now for the sack of flour, my lad,' Victoria called cheerfully to her son but, absorbed in unwinding a portion of the wicker pattern at the side of his chair, Edmund gave no answer.

When the young farmer's wife had first found mouse droppings in the tops of the bags of flour bought at a mill she had been horrified and had proclaimed her disgust to the miller in no uncertain terms.

'Well, ye see, ma'am,' he had explained, 'if I'm pushed for time, like I am at certain seasons, when there's a rush on, the flour lies about for a bit before it's shovelled into the bag, an' it don't matter how I try to get rid of the mice, they're back again afore I've had time to turn me back, like.'

Now, as she opened the bag bought in Alvechurch the previous day, it was a matter of course to clear the tiny black specks from the top layers of flour.

Having made sure it was clear, the young wife took a measure of flour and placed it in the dough skeel, a special trough on legs which stood at the right height for mixing. Then she worked in the moistened yeast with her hands, slapped the whole lump on the wooden lid of the skeel and, shaping it into separate batch loaves, pricked the tops with a fork and left them in front of the fire to rise.

One she pricked with a "B" for Edmund, singing as she did so, 'Pat it and prick it, and mark it with B, and put it in the oven for Baby and me.'

Edmund, knowing the sound, laughed, left his bit of destruction for a moment, and clapped his hands to the tune.

Taking the pot of rain water from the top of the range, Victoria poured it into the large tin bowl on the sink and Edmund's dirty laundry was washed and hung on a line to blow between the trees in the orchard.

As soon as the dough had risen Victoria emptied the oven of the hot embers, swept the bricks clean and with the maul, a hard, flat wooden shovel, she placed the batch of loaves on the bricks and closed the door on them.

When they were ready to come out, brown and appetising, Edmund sniffed the air with delight, holding out his hands for the special loaf baked for him, and having received it, he chewed with relish and a ritual swaying back and forth in his chair.

When John and Old Harry came in for their meal at mid-day the farmer threw a pitiful heap of feathers on the settle.

'That was one which must have been trampled on when that danged train set off the mare yesterday,' he said morosely. 'It can't have been dead long for they were all alive last night.'

'Never mind, it's not died of disease. We'll feather and dress it this afternoon. It'll make us a meal with a bit of bacon,' said his wife evenly. 'We can't afford to be too particular, just now.'

After eating the men sat for a while looking through the weekly journals left behind the day before by Joseph Yeoman.

'I seed the old Queen got a new coach to ride through Lunnon Town,' remarked Old Harry as they got up to go out again.

'Oh, ah,' answered John, 'I reckon her's got a bit of riding back and forth to do, seeing the way Parliament's opening and closing so fast with that there Old Disraeli and Old Gladstone shuffling in and out of office like they were playing a game of musical chairs.'

They went back to their work of hedging and ditching for they found the farmlands neglected and in need of a deal of attention. There was not a field where they could safely leave the sheep until gaps had been filled in and ditches full of stagnant water had been dug out and drained.

The table cleared again Sarah sat and feathered the bantam hen and, dropping the tiny pile of feathers into a large tin bowl, she placed them in the still warm baking oven to be cured.

In the evening the log fire in the sitting room was lighted and the tired men sat on either side of the open hearth dozing on the chimney corner seats and pulling on the tangy tobacco in their clay pipes.

In the kitchen Sarah and Victoria were finishing their day's work. They sat at the table with the little pile of cured feathers spread out on the journals and under the mellow light of the oil lamp they trimmed and cut off sharp ends and quills. Almost falling asleep, Sarah sought and found the unbleached calico pillow case into which Victoria let fall the tiny heap of feathers, to be stored there along with the assorted feathers plucked over the last year from ducks, geese, pigeons and poultry at Cotewood.

'Soon be enough for a new pillow there,' they agreed.

After the bread baking, the meal cooking and the feather curing, two bricks were taken out of the oven and wrapped in flannel for heating the bed upstairs.

Then, for its last service of the day into the kitchen oven went the wood-pile, twigs and bits of wood collected by Harry from under the trees as he made his way from the fields to the house. Wet now, by morning they would be tinder-dry and ready for the day's fire-lighting.

From the log fire in the next room the last embers were shovelled into the copper warming-pan and taken up to the second bed for heating the cold flanelette sheets.

'How are the sheep?' asked Victoria, yawning as she held the candle ready for ascending the stairs to bed.

'One of 'em will be dead by morning, I reckon,' replied John.

'Come on then, maister, we'll have to go out and kill her now afore her dies or ye canna make meat on her,' remarked Old Harry.

Chapter 7

"UP THE HILL"

Barn Field, a meadow rising from the back of the barn to the top of the undulating ridge which ran the whole length along the southern edge of the farmlands, was now ready for the sheep without fear of losing them. Four days hard work had made it safe.

The former tenant having sold up and moved out the previous autumn, no grazing had taken place there through the winter months and the sickly animals had a fair chance of recovery feeding on the clean grass of the well-drained hillside.

The men now turned their attention to the farmyard, the cowhouse being in urgent need of repair in order to accommodate three cows and a calf due to arrive from Shortbridge.

John's father owned only a scattering of sheep on his pastures, the animals being unsuited in large numbers to that part of the county, and fluke had passed them by.

Joseph Yeoman's farm being situated on one side of the Bristol to Birmingham road and in an excellent position for supplying the city markets with meat and milk, he had found it profitable to stock up with a good herd of dual purpose cattle for the provision of his main income through beef and dairy products. Again, the foot and mouth epidemic which had recently hit so many cattle breeders had not touched Shortbridge. He had been fortunate.

At this period there were farms all along the route into the city for, though Birmingham was growing at a fast rate, the suburbs had not yet reached out the strangle hold that was later to press the farms out of existence and at this point they were finding the growth of industry to their financial advantage.

Joseph regularly bought and sold in the markets. But at this time of difficulty for his son, who had been obliged to sell his own stock to raise the money for the rent, he gave John the opportunity to obtain from him, at a reasonable price on credit, the beasts his son needed for replacements. It was these which were expected at Beauchamps and must be adequately housed.

On the first Sunday, seeing John out on the cowshed roof shouting instructions to Harry who was working on the inside of the building, Victoria left Sarah to look after the men, and taking Edmund with her, she set off to find the little chapel "up the hill".

Pushing the wicker bassinet, in which the child was a joyful passenger, his mother took the stony path beneath the oaks and elms that stood beside the track leading westward.

After passing through the first gate, where Edmund waved to the moorhens making their way across a pond surrounded by withy and alder trees, the path followed the edge of a fenced field and the bassinet trundled over a miniature brick-built bridge. This spanned a small stream meandering between the meadowed slopes and hills, and here the young mother stopped to point out to her son the tiny fish darting over the pebbles and sending up little clouds of mud through the crystal clear water.

They went on through a second gate and approaching the third at the top of a slope, passed by an orchard and a garden, and there, standing foursquare behind a mossy lawn was a house built so straight up and down that it appeared to Victoria like a child's drawing, with its Georgian porched doorway in the centre, three storeys of windows on either side and a chimney set dead in the middle of a plain slate roof.

'Rough Green Farm, I suppose,' Victoria remarked to her son, 'but it looks more like "the house that Jack Built".' Edmund, architecturally unaware, looked in the direction to which his mother pointed, and not knowing quite what was expected of him by way of answer, to please her, he waved his hands enthusiastically.

No one from the house responded and they made their way across a farm drive to the fourth gate where they found themselves out on the long road winding up a hill.

Halfway up the hill Victora stopped to take breath. It was hard work pushing the pliable wicker pram over the sharp gravel and wheel ruts and when she came to the first cottage by the side of the road she knocked at the door.

It was opened by a girl of about twelve years of age and behind her pressed a group of younger children, all of whom, including the girl with her hand on the latch, were poorly dressed, and all of them stared in silence at the figures on the doorstep.

'I wondered if I could leave my baby carriage here for about an hour and a half,' Victoria requested. 'It is so difficult pushing it up the hill I should find it easier to carry the baby.'

'Couldn't you leave the babby with us? Us'd look arter 'e.'

'What is your name, my dear?' Victoria asked.

'Ivy, if ye please, missus,' answered the girl.

'Well, Ivy, that is kind of you to offer, but I want to take him with me. If you would just look after the baby carriage for me, I will give you a penny for it, and I should be very grateful for the help.'

'Awright then,' answered the girl, a smile of pleasure lighting up her face at the thought of so easily coming into possession of a coin of her own earning — so much was the value of a penny then.

So Victoria, leaving the bassinet in the charge of the girl called Ivy, took Edmund in her arms and went on up the hill.

At the top of the steep climb she leaned against a gate and, propping her child on the top bar, gazed back across the panorama of mist-clouded fields.

She could see Beauchamps standing in a hollow veiled by the black tracery of the leafless trees. To the north-east of the farm, terrace upon terrace the country-side rose into the distance, each undulation with its shadowy fresco of chestnut, oak, sycamore, ash or elm. Sometimes the trees stood in twos and threes, sometimes in larger groups; in long lines of grey silhouettes against the chequered green pasture land or ploughed red clay ground. It was more beautiful than the country round Cotewood, Victoria thought, even in March, for it was more spacious.

She took Edmund up once more and went on along the ridge. Passing between the brick-built cottages on either side she saw that there were two boot-makers, each with their signs displayed. She saw nothing, however, of the general store, which she had decided must be at the other end of the hamlet.

Coming to a lane signposted "To the Chapel" Victoria turned down the slope past the cottages and a farmhouse, and at last, with aching arms and a sigh of relief, she saw the miniature Wesleyan chapel at the top of four stone steps. Behind a hedge it stood alone within a field, contemplating the spectacular view which stretched before its doors away into the blue distance.

Chapter 8

"THERE WAS A LOVELY LADY"

With Edmund on her arm and holding her long skirts high, Victoria mounted the steps, walked up the tiny path and opened the chapel door.

Inside someone was playing the harmonium and the farmer's wife took a seat in one of the hard, high-backed pews, thankfully set Edmund on her lap and settled down to listen. Not one member of the congregation had yet arrived so she decided that she must be early.

The player finished his piece on the instrument and turned in his seat to see who had entered, for the heavy latch on the door could not fail to be heard as it was lifted and dropped.

He was a tall, dignified man of about thirty years of age and seeing the young woman he smiled and spoke to her with easy directness of manner: 'I haven't seen you here before. If this is your first visit, you are very welcome. Do you like music?'

Victoria nodded: 'Yes. I am used to a harmonium and have often played one in the past.'

On being asked where, she told him that she had been a regular player at the chapel where she and her family had been members before she had married and moved away.

'Come and try this one,' he invited, 'while I hold your child.'

'This is Edmund,' she said. And Edmund, as he was handed to the stranger gazed at him gravely while his mother smiling, sat down and played a voluntary by heart.

'Well done!' appauded the young man. 'Would you like to take it on for the service, if Edmund doesn't object?'

'But you are the player,' Victoria demurred.

'No. As a matter of fact I am here only to help out because the regular harmonium player has been taken ill and is in hospital. I don't live here, though I wish I did. I live on my own in a small apartment nearer to Birmingham where my work is.'

Victoria regarded him thoughtfully.

'I think you could live here if you really wish to,' she said slowly.

'How is that then?'

'We have room for a paying guest in our farm. It might be arranged.'

'You have! May I come sometime and see?'

'You are welcome to come back with me for a meal after the service.'

'I will be most glad to accept an invitation from such a lovely lady,' he answered gallantly.

He introduced himself as Roger Comptney, accountant. Then there was no more conversation for the door of the chapel opened loudly, two old people entered and made their way slowly to a front pew.

'Play another voluntary while I go and watch for the preacher,' suggested Roger Comptney.

The young mother knew several musical pieces by heart and found no difficulty in complying with his request. More of the congregation began to drift slowly into their accustomed places, greeting one another loudly as they latched and unlatched the door at each entry.

Through the little mirror standing on the harmonium top Victoria watched them find their seats, the men who were farmers dressed in their black Sunday best, some of the labourers in clean smocks, while the wives wore white aprons under worsted capes or shawls, and bonnets, a little out of date, over their curls. The colours worn by the women were all either brown, grey or black, for since the Prince Consort had died twenty years before, this was still the fashion set by the Victoria on the throne.

The preacher arrived and was introduced to the Victoria on the harmonium seat, who was then presented to the congregation as 'This lovely lady who is going to play for us this morning.'

The service had proceeded as far as the second hymn when the latch was lifted and a farm labourer walked heavily down the aisle to the two old people at the front, where he bent down and spoke loudly into the old man's ear.

"The lovely lady", confused by the sudden, somewhat noisy interruption immediately behind her, stopped playing. For a moment the congregation under the impetus of the tune's rhythm, carried on singing without accompaniment, then hesitated and came to a stop, except for one voice.

Roger Comptney sang on alone in a mellifluous, baritone voice to which everyone listened. Some, at the front, turning round to look, saw the singer sitting in his pew with a little child upon his lap who stared open-mouthed at the strange person smiling and singing at one and the same time. Others fixed their gaze on the preacher in the pulpit as though he were personally responsible for producing the voice from heaven in their midst.

In the middle of it all the old man shuffled out behind his labourer, dropping the door latch like the report of a gun.

Edmund's mother had no sooner gathered her wits about her and commenced playing again, when the old man returned, walked heavily down the aisle and in turn bent down to his wife's ear and said for all to hear:

'The key!'

His wife, answering in a high quavering voice, said:

'Speak up, can't ye, Ebenezer, 'ow d'ye reckon I can hear what you be a'saying, when you speak in that whisper o' yourn?'

The old man repeated his request on a louder note. The old woman fished in her pockets for the needed object and her husband stumped up the aisle to the door while the congregation sang lustily, finishing the remaining verses unaccompanied, since Victoria, again mystified by events had ceased to play. The congregation sat down with self-congratulatory smiles at having coped with the situation satisfactorily.

The service proceeded with no more interruptions. When it was over the harmonium player apologised to the preacher for the breaks in her playing, but he and Roger Comptney assured her that something always happened in the services which had not been planned; everyone took this for granted and carried on as if all were normal.

Then, with Roger carrying Edmund, they made their way downhill again, Victoria having promised to play at the service whenever she was needed and without breaking down at any future interruptions.

When they came to the cottage the door was opened before they knocked, and the bassinet pushed out to them.

'Is that yer 'usband?' enquired Ivy.

Victoria blushed and explained hastily: 'No, my dear, it's a friend who is very kindly helping me by carrying my heavy baby for me.'

When they came near to Beauchamps, Roger said, 'I know this place. I've passed it when out riding.'

Chapter 9

THE VISITORS

Leaving Edmund asleep in the wicker pram beneath the trees, Victoria took Roger Comptney round the garden to the farmyard where John was still at work with Harry on the roof of the cowhouse.

After introductions and explanation she left the men together and almost before she had time to hang up her cloak, Roger had knocked at the back door, entered and borrowed an old coat of John's to replace his own. This he flung on the back of the settle and was out again to help the two men.

Victoria had a "conflab" with Sarah about the right room to set the guest for his meal.

Before making her decision, Sarah stepped out to the pump and, while drawing water, watched the men at work. Coming back with the pail she said to her mistress: 'You cast yer eyes on them men out there, missus. If ye put any on 'em in the best room them'll stink the place out after bein' in that there cowshed!'

In honour of the guest the least that could be done, and the most it seemed, was to replace the usual tin every-day mugs with the pewter tankards for the cider which would inevitably follow the meal.

When they came in for dinner, hunger assuaged, the men took out their pipes, filled them, and talking began as the fragrant smoke spiralled upwards and filled the room with the pungent odour which encouraged men's conversation.

Turning to Harry with a direct question, Comptney asked: 'What do you think of Joseph Arch?'

'Oh-ah, 'e's a fine upstanding feller to lead the young uns,' answered Harry, 'but risen up too late for the likes of me. Good luck to un, I says though, if he can get a fairer deal for us labourers so much the better. Beggin the maister's pardon, fer I reckon he ben't noways better off'n a labourer as things stand.'

John Yeoman sent a quick look of guilt in the direction of his wife, but Victoria, if she were aware of it, did not look up from the sink where she and Sarah were washing the dishes.

Roger Comptney, watching the farmer with a keen eye, turned back to the old labourer.

'I tell you, Harry, that Jo Arch before he's finished will be in the Government and getting the vote for the men in the country just as the town workers have it now. And then no matter how old you are you'll need to have your opinion about things. If you had the vote now for whom would you use it?'

Harry was nothing if not a realist. 'What's the use of astin that now?' he enquired. 'It'm be a year or two afore that comes off and there'll be a different set of folks in the Gov'ment be then, and another man at work here, I can tell ye. But I be willun to bet ye this: whoever's at work on the farm in my place'll do the same as wot I would. He'd vote fer the man who had the poor in mind and who'd do most fer 'em.'

23

'Well spoken, man,' applauded Comptney, heartily. 'Now what do you say, John Yeoman?'

'I say,' answered the young farmer, putting his pipe on the table and bending forward to glare fiercely into Roger's face. 'I say,' and he slammed his clenched fist down as he spoke, 'that if us farmers had fairer tenancy agreements, easier rates and rents, and what's more, no danged tythes to pay to a church we don't support; oh-ah, and something else that no man can do anything about - better weather - we should have the money to pay the labourers the fairer wage that is their due!' All the pent-up bitterness of the last two years came pouring out and Comptney looked at him in silence, drawing thoughtfully on his pipe. He hardly noticed that Victoria had left the room to attend to Edmund, and Sarah had stumped slowly up the stairs to the room above the kitchen.

John, with a face as black as thunder, resumed his tirade against the conditions of his life.

'And lookye at this danged Royal Commission Disraeli sent out to look into the agricultural depression. What does it do? It asks ye a lot of danged silly questions about how much capital ye've got, if any!' Roger nodded sympathetically and John, encouraged, went on.

'How much ye spend and what ye spend it on! Prying into ye private affairs, that's all it is. Well, they won't get anything out of me, I can tell ye.' He thumped the table again. Roger raised his eyebrows.

'And I can tell ye this,' John raged. 'The Tories do it to get the Tories back in power. Votes for the Tories! Votes for the Liberals! Huh! They're all as bad as one another. I tell you, Harry, and ye can take it from me, the man who looks after the poor the best is the man who does it to keep his party in power!

Roger Comptney took his pipe out of his mouth and said, 'Oh, come now, John Yeoman, there are some men of principle, you know.'

'You show me the man and I'll vote for him, when I get the chance!' John spoke in rank scorn. 'D'ye know what that chap Disraeli said?'

'It depends on the statement to which you are referring,' Roger answered.

Before John had time to answer there was a sound like a sudden storm of hailstones on the ceiling above their heads.

'What was that?' Roger asked, looking out of the window for indication of weather conditions.

Harry said, knocking his pipe out on the bars of the range fire, 'Eh, that be only me old woman upstairs turning herself about to get comf'table for her forty winks in the wicker chair. Ah, and I'll be orf t'yon cowshed to finish me job there.' He stood up, took an old sack from behind the door, drew it round his shoulders and hobbled out on his rheumaticky legs. He had no intention of listening to any more of "they politics".

'Well,' went on Roger, settling again; though every now and then his eyes strayed on to the ceiling as another sound reached his ears, that of a long indrawn 'Hoomph...' followed by an expelled 'paaah...' which he concluded was old Sarah, now "comf'table", snoring. 'Go on.' He encouraged his companion.

24

'I'm meaning that speech Disraeli made at that Agricultural Dinner,' said John, working up again. 'He said that there was one party which was setting labourer agin farmer, and tenant agin landlord for a political purpose of their own, so he says, in order to get rid of the "aristocrazy" in favour of the "democrazy". As far as I'm concerned the whole danged lot are crazy!'

'Put like that I could sometimes agree with you!' laughed Roger.

From above there came a louder than usual 'Hoom-pah' followed by the sound of hailstorm and a clumping of footsteps signifying the end of old Sarah's ration of "winks".

Victoria came back down the passage with Edmund on her arm, fed and happy, and as Sarah came to the bottom of the stairs from her room, the child was passed over to her welcoming arms.

'John,' said his wife, 'there's a fine carriage with a pair of greys at the front gate. It must be someone special visiting us.'

John went through to the front porch to see who it was that could be visiting them so soon and so grandly.

Through the glassed half of the front door he could see the matching grey horses shaking their heads as the reins were held loosely by a coachman who, seated on the driving dickey of a well turned out carriage, sat looking about him.

A tall, somewhat stern-faced man in his late thirties opened the white painted iron gate, whose hinges, even after oiling, always worked up that sharp octave of sound that only iron hinges can give, a distinctive, unforgettable sound remembered with affection by all who passed through.

A lady, dressed in fashionable town clothes followed and closing the gate after her, listened to the downward octave.

As he opened the door John recognised them. It was his landlord Charles Bennet and his wife, and they came down the path greeting their tenant genially. Victoria, following behind, was introduced, and after talking for a few minutes on the path they all made their way through to the sitting room, taking their seats before the blazing log fire.

Roger was called to join the company and the two young Yeomans were surprised to see Comptney greet the newcomers with friendly familiarity.

'My solicitor,' explained the accountant, and added jokingly, 'he keeps me on the straight and narrow path both in my business and my private life.'

'Roger is always welcome as a friend in our house,' said Mrs. Bennet, 'for our families have known each other for many years.' She was about the same age as her husband with any easy, vivacious manner that pleased the farmer's wife.

Roger explained his presence, which brought the conversation to a central point around which an immediate discussion took place.

'Now this is the reason for our early visit,' Charles Bennet began. 'The old tenant has gone, fresh blood is here and the farm needs pulling together again.'

His wife smiled and nodded to Victoria, but the latter listened in some trepidation, well knowing her husband's down-right and sometimes tactless manner.

John Yeoman fulfilled her expectations immediately, answering the landlord abruptly and with blunt speech:

'Maybe fresh blood is here, Mr. Bennet, and maybe you have your ideas about what needs doing. But as a solicitor you will know there are two sides to every question and, before we discuss anything you may want to do, there are certain things I want to be clear about.'

'Let's hear them,' suggested Charles Bennet in a matter-of-fact tone.

'On my side, Mr. Bennet, I want to know first and foremost if my tenure is secure. You speak of bringing the farm up to standard, and from what I can see it is going to take a deal of effort and money to do that.' His landlord nodded and said, 'Go on.'

'I have just left a farm,' he went on, 'where for two years I worked like a slave, putting all I had into the repair and improvement it needed. My wife will tell you that I am not afraid of hard work and I wanted to see that farm good, for it was our first. Now, on top of the bad luck with sheep fluke, as soon as that farm was in fit condition the landlord gave us notice to quit.' John stopped to re-light his pipe, then continued.

'Mr. Bennet, you are a solicitor, not a farmer. You may own the land but do you know and understand any of the present conditions that have brought us small farmers so low that we have to sell our stock to get the rent in time for Quarter Day? My last landlord used the fact that I wasn't breaking even as an excuse to get me out because he wanted the place for a member of his own family. He was moving in to reap what I had sown. Is that your reason for bringing in "fresh blood" to pull the farm together?'

John's voice had increased in depth and volume as resentment welled up within him and, with his characteristic gesture when roused, he rose to his feet and thumped the table with his palm.

Victoria looked uneasily at the solicitor's wife, but undisturbed that lady gave her a reassuring smile and place her hand gently over Victoria's to calm her.

Charles Bennet looked grave and when he spoke his voice was stern. 'Mr. Yeoman, I see your point. I do know and realise the depressed conditions that exist in agriculture at this present time'. He rose to his feet, walked across the room and looked out of the window at the parkland stretching northward from the house. Then he spoke again.

'I did not turn out the last tenant because of the condition he had allowed the farm to fall into, though I would have been in my rights to have done so. He was an old man and his son came and persuaded him to give up the tenancy because the farm was too much for him. Michaelmas had come and gone before he moved out but I asked for no more rent for the extra time he was here. Beyond that you have Roger here to testify to the kind of person I am and the kind of landlord I am likely to be.'

Roger Comptney looked at the farmer, who was sitting down again. Then he gave his testimony.

I can assure, Yeoman, a straighter man you'll not find if you are straight with him. And if I am any judge of character, which I pride myself on being, I am sure you are a fair-minded one.'

'Right,' said John, somewhat mollified. 'And I hear you are a Quaker so I'm bound to take your word for it.'

Roger smiled at the implied compliment both to himself and his religion. Then the farmer resumed.

'Now the next thing is that I want you to see my present position clearly, then we can all be in the straight.'

He explained it fully while the visitors listened with a quiet receptive attitude that allayed Victoria's fears about her husband's truculence; and that gave the farmer a chance to revise his ideas about landlords, who evidently were not all the same!

'Well now, if you do your part, I think we can help you in several ways,' said Charles Bennet. 'Tell them, Constance.'

His wife said quietly. 'You have told us that Roger wants to come and live here as a paying guest and I am sure my husband will not object to that, since we want to do something similar. We would like you to keep two rooms for us to use at weekends for as long as we require them, and we would adjust the rent accordingly.'

Victoria looked across at her husband and he nodded. 'That's just what would help us more than anything, Mrs. Bennet, for as you know we have more rooms than we need for our own use,' she answered.

So it was settled there and then, and while the farmer's wife took Roger Comptney and the landlord's wife to see the rooms that were available, John Yeoman, with a smoother temper and a calmer manner perused the tenancy agreement with his landlord. Then they both went out to look over the farmstead together and to discuss what materials and payment for repairs would be necessary.

Charles Bennet said: 'We shall want to do some shooting with friends at the weekends and you are welcome to join us whenever you care to. But did you know, Yeoman, that this year it becomes legal for tenants to shoot ground game on the land they farm?'

'That's not until the autumn - is it?' John had seen something about it in Berrow's Journal but, with all the hassle of moving, his depression over the sheep, the general state of his affairs and his opinion of landlords, it had escaped his attention.

Now - he thought he might be on the verge of revising that last opinion. May be - but only may be, mind, he would have to wait and see - there might be some reasonable landlords.

Chapter 10

THE HOUSE

Climbing the centuries old stairway with its time-blackened banisters and crossing the uneven floor boards of the old landing, Victoria Yeoman opened a door whose latch must have been lifted for a variety of purposes, some innocent, some nefarious over a period of at least three hundred years.

As another flight of narrow stairs of equal antiquity was revealed Roger Comptney remarked with a note of interested speculation 'You know this seems to be just the place where you could run into a monk!"

Victoria turned to look at him. 'It's curious that you should say that,' she replied, 'for I always feel the sense of a monkish presence whenever I am treading these stairs or walking through the porch below.' She stepped aside to allow her two companions to ascend to the attic.

At the top of the staircase Roger Comptney stood riveted, drawing in his breath with delight at the sight of the strangely beautiful double room before him. It was divided into two compartments not by walls or screens but by the positions of the joists, huge trunks of jet black, some of which lay horizontally across the sloping floor, others, as though growing there, rising vertically or diagonally to the angled roof.

Mrs. Bennet, equally impressed, though it was not the first time she had seen it, stepped over a massive beam and walked across to one of the small windows to peer through the panes. 'You know, before your monks took over, Roger, I think this land must have been a king's deer park, and Beauchamps its lodge,' she observed.

To reach a second window Comptney found himself stepping up to a floor a couple of feet higher than that in the compartment where the solicitor's wife stood gazing at her favourite view. He noted three windows and murmured to himself, 'From this apartment it must be possible to see every side of the farm except the orchard to the west.' He looked down over the monastic porch toward the iron gate behind which the landlord's carriage waited. Beyond that he could see the rickyard and barn, the duck-pond, and the Barn Field rising upwards to the ridge on the sky-line.

From the third window Roger looked down on the farmyard where tenant and landlord were examining the structure of the farm buildings and where Harry was at work on the cowhouse walls.

Victoria, who loved this upper part of the house, was still standing at the door and, holding it with one hand, she ran the palm of the other over the raised lines of the carving, as though she herself had been the workman at its making, but was blind and must know its quality by touch.

She walked up the stairs in a trance and, forgetting her companions' presence, reached out to the first great upright beam extending her arms around its black girth as though to embrace a lover, and indeed the action represented the deep emotion the room aroused in her. She said aloud, 'Someone, I am sure, has lived a lifetime in this room.'

Roger Comptney turned from the window. 'Someone may have done,' he agreed. 'These are the kind of farms which could have belonged to the monastery, when it still existed, which was only a matter of about three miles away from here. The farms were called granges and were often used for recalcitrant monks who were sent to live and work out a penance by farming the monastery lands.' His eyes twinkled. 'The role of recalcitrant monk would just suit me, Mrs. Yeoman, and if my friends do not require this apartment, this is what I would choose to live in.'

The landlord's wife walked from her window and said 'You shall, Roger, for I have my eye on that large ground floor room with French windows facing the parkland and another which I think will take your fancy just as much as this has done.'

They stepped carefully down the ancient stairway in single file and Victoria closed the door separating that old, serene, beamed world from the rest of the house.

Mrs. Bennet had already gone past the open door of the next room without stopping. 'There's something about the atmosphere of that room I don't like,' she explained. 'It has a strange, suffocating, secretive feel about it that makes me shiver.'

Roger looked at it. All he could see was a long narrow room with whitewashed walls and a dark uneven floor. 'Maybe the window is small for the size of the room,' he suggested. Then he added: 'But rooms do seem to have personalities of their own sometimes, and for that matter houses also. This house certainly has a profoundly interesting and complex character built up for it by Old Father Time and by circumstances and events of the past.'

Victoria went to the window and threw it open to the keen March air to rid the room of its musty smell. I wonder who has occupied this to make it so unpleasant a place? she wondered to herself. I'll make it the general toilet closet.

Following the others through the door opposite she heard Roger Comptney exclaim: 'Fine bit of work this, Constance!'

'I agree. You could almost say that this was the item that decided us when we came to buy the property.'

The room was solid oak from floor to ceiling, with finely worked wainscotting along each wall. Nothing, other than time, seemed to have touched it since the day it was created from the wood whose darkening hue enabled it to withstand the erosion of the centuries with a calm serenity.

A lovely small-paned window broke the line of the oak on the north wall and the viewers looked out on a full grown cedar which spread its majestic branches across a corner of the lawn. A wide but rough wagon-track wound between the stately elms and oaks of the parkland and disappeared into the distance where it met the road between the hamlet of Rowney Green and the village of Alvechurch.

Mrs. Bennet walked round the walls tapping the panels. 'I don't know about your monk farmers, Roger, but I am sure that if this place has been a king's lodge in a deer park, there surely can't be a room like this without a secret opening in the panels,' she said. 'I tried it the first time I came round it, but nothing moves beneath my exploring fingers. Yet the room seems almost to call out for something to be found here.'

'If this is to be your room you will be able to spend all your weekends searching,' teased Roger, 'and you can let us know when you find what is hidden here.'

As they made their way down the stairs again they passed the four steep steps that led from the main staircase to the room occupied by Victoria Yeoman and her husband.

'There's another peculiar thing,' remarked Mrs. Bennet, 'in that room you have chosen for yourselves. It's a sunny cheerful room but it has that odd little half-sized door which is only the height of a child. You have to bend double to pass through it into the next room, the long one over the kitchen occupied by your two old servants. Can you imagine what was its use?'

'It is odd,' agreed Victoria. 'I have wondered myself, and the only guess I have been able to make is that it might have been made for a child to pass through from a parent's room to a Nannie's, for Sarah and Harry's room would be suitable for such a purpose.'

But Roger had another solution. As they stood at the bottom of the stairs they were facing a tiny room with its oak door open and with a lattice window looking out on to the passage running between the sitting room and the front door.

'How singular!' exclaimed Mrs. Bennet. 'Why should a minute room like that want not only two windows built into the outer walls but one on the inside as well?'

Roger was peering into the room. 'There's a trap door in the floor which I suppose opens over the cellars?' he queried.

'That's right,' answered the farmer's wife, 'and one set of steps leading down and another set leading up and out on to the garden path, so that cider barrels can be taken down from outside the house, but tapped and brought up inside the house.'

'H'm.' said Roger thoughtfully. 'And other things as well, I reckon.' He turned back to the stairs and closely examined them, then he straightened his back and said. 'Just as I thought! Look at this.' He pointed to a spot in the upright of a stair, and the two women eyeing it closely, could see that there was a faint circle.

'I think there might once have been an eyehole in that stair, blocked in now, but it could be that there was a hiding place beneath those stairs through which an eye would look straight into that little room, watching who could be coming up the steps from the cellar, watching what goes on, unseen and unknown. And that little half-door upstairs suggests that there was a time when this house hid a secret danger, for in any search carried out through the rooms only one person at a time could crawl through that half-size door and doubled up at that! You were right, Constance. Someone once had something or someone to hide here! What a tale this house could tell if it had a voice!'

'Ah, well,' said Victoria, as the two parties met again in the sitting room, with its heavily beamed ceiling and wide open hearth, 'it has a new tale to tell now.'

As the farmer and his wife watched the departure of the landlord, accompanied by his wife and their friend, Roger Comptney, John Yeoman said enviously: 'Those matching greys! I wish they were mine!'

Victoria answered teasingly: 'Thou shalt not covet thy neighbour's goods, nor his wife, nor his asses.'

Her husband replied: 'No. But the Ten Commandments said nothing about his greys!'

Chapter 11

THE FARM

Three weeks later Roger Comptney arrived at Beauchamps with a van full of furniture for the attic apartment.

The van driver tied up his horse in the yard and left him with a nose-bag while he and his mate hauled chairs, tables, a bed and a bookcase up the stairs, removing legs to manoeuvre difficult pieces up the narrow top staircase, screwing them back into place when the two-storeyed floor was reached; after which the men departed leaving the accountant to clear up the remaining muddle of books and pictures.

When all was in order with his books in place and water-colours and old prints showing well on the white-washed walls Roger called down the stairs to Victoria to come up and give her approval.

Little does he know, thought the farmer's wife, as she stood back and viewed the double apartment with satisfaction, that those curtains in the windows have been made from my second best poplin dress skirt! But they look good and will look even better in lamp-light.

She had not been able to afford to buy the material for the purpose and she knew that John would never notice what had gone into the sewing. The curtains were a rich warm purple, the brightest colour she could put her hands on, for most of her dresses were in the sombre shades of the current fashion. To make the curtains even brighter to the eye she had feather-stitched two heavy lines across the bottom hem with double strands of wine red silk.

The rest of the week-end Roger spent in the farmyard giving John and Harry a hand with the repair of the stables, one of which housed the two farm horses (one borrowed) and the mare. The other was intended for the future accommodation of Bennet's horses and the hunter Comptney had in mind for the provision of his own means of transport.

By the second week-end Comptney had obtained a handsome black and yellow gig which he left under cover in the open cowshed along the fore-draught, used, not to house cows since there were so few, but to shelter other farm vehicles and implements.

By the third week-end he had his hunter, a sleek and polished chestnut gelding named Sheikh, with Arab blood in his veins. Sheikh's days in the hunting field were finished but he was in good enough condition to do the work of drawing a light gig and carrying a rider over the fields in leisurely fashion, without the exertion of racing hell for leather after the hunt.

'Eh, he's a bit like me!' was Joseph Yeoman's comment on his condition.

Now able to live wholly at Beauchamps Roger Comptney drove daily to the station, Sheikh being taken by a lad to a nearby farm where his owner had an agreement with the farmer to graze him in one of his fields, the latter having the use of the horse as payment for his keep.

The first drive in the gig for pleasure was on the following Sunday when Roger took Victoria and Edmund to the chapel "up the hill".

Ivy, watching as they passed the cottage, said to her brothers and sisters: 'Her wunna leave her baby carriage here no more. Her's a grand lady riding past now!' Ivy, with her Brummagem accent had no use for "H's" in her speech, and she turned her soft "a" sounds into "i's", her "ows" into "aioo" so that the sentence above is a translation of her real speech.

It was a month later when the Bennets arrived, driven over in their carriage by the coachman and he, having helped with the third upheavel of furniture removal into the house, returned to Birmingham with the carrier who had brought the furniture, leaving his employer to drive back in his own time.

That Sunday was another gala day for the young Yeomans.

When Victoria took in the Bennet's breakfast, Mrs. Bennet said to her: 'We usually go into Birmingham for Sunday worship, and like you we are Non-conformists. This time we would like to join you at your chapel "up the hill". Will you accompany us in the carriage? We would be so pleased if we could all go together this once.'

Victoria could hardly believe her eyes when she saw that John was getting his work done in time — and for what? She found it even more incredible when she saw him mount the driving seat of the carriage and take the reins as coachman to his landlord. And John himself found it difficult to believe that it was happening.

Old Sarah stood at the back door with her hands on her hips and ejaculated: 'Well, my eye! Wonders will never cease!' And Old Harry watching from the cowhouse said: 'Well an'din't I say there be landlords an' landlords!'

When Ivy saw such grandeur driving past the cottage she said to her little family, whose noses were pressed against the window. 'Eh! That's not our Mrs. Yeoman a-waving to us. That's the Queen a-riding by with the young prince on her lap, and her Lidy-in-Witing asoide her. Her'll not never lave her biby carrige here again.' (Partially translated)

That first spring John Yeoman's father and his youngest brother, William, came over every week to Beauchamps to help with the late ploughing, the swift sowing and planting; by working solidly from early light to nightfall they were able to achieve more than John had expected.

The members of both households were so exhausted when the day's toil was finished that they threw themselves on their beds and falling asleep at once, awoke in the morning to find that they had not removed their clothes. There was one advantage in this — it saved the energy of dressing again.

The Bennets travelled over each week-end in a sporty tandem carriage and when not out riding with his wife and friends the landlord was not averse to putting his hand to a hoe between the growing rows of beans and peas.

'Eh, John,' he said, 'when I get between those straight lines after a week's work with some crooked clients it gives me back my sense of balance. And I can tell you this: fetching weeds out of the ground is a deal easier than getting the truth out of some of 'em!'

Roger Comptney, needing fresh air after the daily grind of calculations in the city, of an evening was also out in farmyard or fields, for he came to love every activity that took place on the farmstead.

He even went as far as attempting to remove the blue-fly maggots from under the mucked wool round the sheep's rumps, though before he was able to do this he found that it was necessary to have the farmer teach him how to catch and hold the animal. He had discovered that there was an art, a science and a technique involved in the simplest work of the agricultural industry.

Once again that summer was as wet as ever. The grass and clover crops were late and lay discoloured under soaking rain for days before the swathes could be turned for drying out. The hay did not turn black, however, as in the previous year at Cotewood, and at last it was voted ready for carrying.

Then, snatching the few fine days available to them, the whole household turned out with the hay-wain, rakes and pitchforks. Roger joined them in the evening and the Bennets at the week-end, while Edmund was left to crawl and totter in the hay near the hedge, watched over by Cadger, a stray sheep-dog who had been found picking food from the rubbish dump, and who had never left again.

With John on top loading and Old Harry leading the horses it was not long before there was a steaming rick which caused the farmer as much worry up as down, because of the risk of fire breaking from the damp hot centre.

His father brought over his rick tester and every day John thrust the lengthy pronged iron rod into the rick for a sample of hay from the area where the trouble could arise, and as soon as he was able he thatched the rick, for once that was done he learnt he might be able to insure it.

The corn, likewise late, was difficult to cut because some of the crop had been flattened by heavy rain and thunderstorms during July, but this was not unusual, and at least it had not been entirely spoiled as in the year before. The yield, though poor in quality and quantity could be taken to the miller in Alvechurch and when ground there was enough to keep them in bread for some time to come. 'We shan't starve yet,' was Victoria's assessment of the situation.

John, depressed because they seemed to be making no headway, remarked to his wife one day as they began to pick the fruit in the orchard, 'My name ought to be "Calamity Job" I reckon, for this year isn't much better than the last. Who could have thought that the bad weather would go on for so long, seemingly for ever.' An apple fell and he looked down at it.

'Remember the sunny days we used to have when we were children, Vic? The scent of the hay came sweet across my father's fields and the corn went to mill and market. We had enough then for our own use for the whole year.'

'Yes,' answered Victoria, 'we remember the sunny days. What we forget are the times of rain and the gusty weather. I suppose it will always be the same, when our children are grown, folks'll say just the same. They'll forget the bad old times of the past, thinking them all good because they don't like the time they have in the present. And now, my lad, count your blessings.' And she proceeded to list them for him as she sorted the apples he brought her:

'1. You've got a good landlord.

2. A reasonable rent.

3. Regular income from paying guests.

4. The sheep have picked up and this autumn will be strong enough for a ram.

5. We can eat as many rabbits as we like without having to poach them from the land we work.

6. The cows have given a good yield and the milk is selling.

7. My butter, homemade cakes, jam etc. is selling in the market.

8. This orchard fruit is excellent and there'll be enough cider and perry for ourselves and maybe the market as well.

9. This morning I saw a field full of mushrooms waiting for the picking.'

John said, as he lowered the brimful bucket from the tree he had been working: 'Oh — ah, ye're right, me wench, but I can't help wondering if I'm going to make it, with everything so much on the balance. One small extra and we might be on the rocks again.'

Victoria said nothing to this, but she thought the more. The one "small extra" was already on its way and she wondered whether it would be a son or a daughter. From the point of view of economy a son would be a blessing in two directions. Edmund's clothes could be handed down to a boy for one thing. For another if John did pull the farm round on to an even keel and make a go of it, as she felt in her bones he would, then later on another son would be a great help.

Anyway, she thought, others had found their way through difficult times with far more than one "little extra" so why shouldn't they? She was not afraid of either hard work or the future — and then there were those mushrooms. They were an unexpected bonus which neither of them had taken into account. She wouldn't be surprised if they tipped the balance in the right direction.

Chapter 12

MISFORTUNES

Previous to Charles Bennet becoming landlord of Beauchamps the farmstead had been owned by the widow of an old friend and client of his.

She had been in the habit of visiting the farm twice a year, Lady Day and Michaelmas, to collect the rent and keep an eye on the property, at the same time enjoying the slow drive through the country-side in spring and autumn.

Charles Bennet had once accompanied the old lady on one of these trips and had been immediately attracted to the surrounding landscape through which they passed, to the old house and its still beautiful parkland.

The estate also included Rough Green Farm, though this was a much later building of simple Georgian practicality, whose outer appearance had suggested to Victoria the idea of a child's drawing.

Now approaching his prime, the solicitor, a man of wide interests, at once became concerned with the current position and problems of agriculture, seeing them at first hand in the work of the farm throughout that summer.

It was when he saw his tenants, or one of the old servants, pumping water from the well at the back door, or at the sink pump in the kitchen, drawing soft water from the rain storage tank below the kitchen floor, that he found his attention drawn to the farm's water supply.

He could not help being concerned that the drinking water came from the outside well, not because it meant going outside in all weathers, but because of the possibility of contamination from the farmyard whose muck was washed down by every fall of rain into the sub-soil only a yard or two away, with the likelihood, in all the wet weather of the recent summers, of seepage into the well.

He noted that the rain water from the storage tank was used for both cooking and washing purposes, and though under present conditions the store was adequate, should there come a fine summer that supply could dry up and disappear.

'I'm going to make a complete tour of the land round the two farmsteads,' the landlord said to his wife, 'would you like to come with me?'

Together they walked the fields searching for springs and at last, walking down the hill from the southern ridge, they came upon one near the bottom, feeding the little stream which flowed eventually under the bridge over which Victoria walked with Edmund on her way to chapel.

'Excellent,' said Bennet.

'Will it do?' asked his wife.

'Couldn't be better! It's exactly half-way between the two farms and a deep one by its position.'

Without delay he went about finding the most suitable method of using the flow. The result was the installation of a Hydraulic Ram, a system devised early in the century for the mechanical pumping of spring water through pipes to the house requiring a supply.

Serving both Beauchamps and Rough Green Farm, by the end of that summer, water poured into the respective kitchens by way of a bright new, gleaming brass tap at each sink.

The man responsible for this innovation went to the taps in turn and, sampling the sparkling liquid that emerged, announced that it was good.

Sarah, in the kitchen at Beauchamps, hearing his pronouncement turned to look at him, awestruck for a moment. Then she said: 'Oh — ah, that's what God said when his work on the world was done, but it turned out he were wrong, dint it? He said as much isself, dint he? And nearly washed the 'ole thing out! Us a'gotter wait and see wi' this here new fangled contraption, ent us? All that glisters inna gold, ye know!' And with this dire warning she gave the brass tap a significant look.

One cold morning in November the old servant came clumping down the stairs to fetch the family's water for early toilet.

She went to the range, poked out the ashes, relit the fire with sticks from the wood-pile pushed into the still hot cinders and, taking the big kettle over to the sink, turned on the brass tap. No water came through it.

She turned it further, off, then on again; pushed her gnarled finger up its spout; still no water from it.

'New fangled notions, wot did Oi sy! Oi were roight weren't Oi? Us knows summat, us old uns, any road. Gorn sorft these young uns, and when folks go sorft un gets the trouble un asts for!' Sarah muttered to herself and went back to the familiar old pump.

When the water was ready she took the shepherd's crook from behind the back door and banged on the ceiling and the bottom stair.

There was a shuffling from above. Sarah mounted half-way and waited for her husband to come that far down the stairs, then gave him two cans of warm water to place at the half-size door.

Old Harry took them, knocked on the door and waited for the muffled answer from within which satisfied him that someone had heard.

When the "maister and missus" were down, Sarah made known the situation regarding the recalcitrant brass tap, remarking as she did so, 'Oh — ah, Oi said the owuld ways might turn out to be the best in the long run, din't Oi? Us'll have to go back to 'em now!' She carried her words into action by throwing her shawl around her shoulders, and picking up the water bucket she clattered out to the pump and worked it vigorously, like the warm shaking of an old friend's hand.

John did not wait for breakfast but drank quickly from a jug kept filled in the dairy with ice-cold water. From the table he grabbed half a batch loaf, put on his boots while chewing it and ate the remainder as he made his way across the orchard and fields to the shed which housed the ram.

An autumn mist hung low across the fields below him and swathed the southern ridge above, while his boots left pale foot-prints in the white rime of the first frost upon the land. His breath blew out in steamy rivulets to join the sea of fog around him and he gazed intently toward Rough Green Farm, hoping to see the form of Hubert English materialise out of the insubstantial landscape, making his way to the same mecca as himself, for it did not occur to him that whatever trouble lay within the ram may not have stopped the tap running at the second farm.

He could see nothing but the dim outlines of gates and hedges and the disembodied ghosts of trees, some with only the crowns visible, others with only trunks attached to unreal ground, and as he drew near the ram house with the climbing land behind it and the tiny chatter of the stream below, he became as puzzled as Sarah had been at the non-flowing tap.

He could hear something he had not expected, that regular pumping sound of a healthily working mechanism, as though the earth possessed a heart beat of its own but with water circulating through its veins instead of blood. Could the thing have righted itself while he was on his way there?

Then he realised that it was not the normal full sound that could usually be heard. As he drew level with the shed he became aware of a noise above the gurgling of the brook and saw a running flood of water escaping across the gravel and grass to the stream below.

He opened the door, saw that one cylinder was working perfectly, the one serving Rough Green Farm, but from the one supplying Beauchamps came the flood that was pouring down the field.

John, never having had to deal with a fault such as this before, felt at a loss. He tried to remember all that Charles Bennet had shown him when explaining the mechanism, and recalled his words: 'If anything goes wrong, try the simplest thing first. A small fault can sometimes cause a complete stoppage.'

He put down his tools and unbolting the inspection plate put his hand inside to feel round the valve for any obstruction. The freezing water took most of the sensation from his hand except for that of aching cold, but — yes — there was a small object wedged against the valve, preventing it from performing its normal function of opening and closing, and the water, instead of passing through in a rhythmic, intermittent flow, was gushing out.

John removed the object, a pebble, and bolted on the plate again. He watched. The usual pleasant rhythm of the machine's correct motion under the force and impetus of the moving column of water had recommenced.

Yeoman could hardly believe it. Ah, well, perhaps it would not always be so simple, and as he was thinking this he heard another quite different sound, nothing to do with the ram.

Hah! thought John, the season's begun. He stepped out of the ram house and straightening his back, found that the mist had lifted.

Then along the length of the southern ridge against the background of sky he saw the hounds in full cry, and ahead of them the fox streaking westwards across the fields.

Before the huntsman and followers appeared he could hear the reverberations of the thundering hooves on the other side of the hill. Then there they were, red and black, tan and black silhouettes riding the length of the ridge edged with shining gold against the sunlit sky.

Nearer at hand there was a loud, excited neigh. Patch, the farm horse, had been grazing in the field just this side of the ridge and the next minute, lifting his head high, he let out another scream of intoxication and was racing along the hedge-side in a determined attempt to join the hunt.

Arriving at the far end of the field in time to see the cavalcade careering past immediately in front of him, he became so enthralled that in his attempt to join in he set himself at the fence and running at it with heavy thuds he jumped.

He was not a hunter but a half-legged horse, that is, an animal bred from a heavy breed on one side of the parentage and a light breed on the other, a multi-purpose horse, having gone hunting but with little jumping experience. In the stimulation of the event he cleared the fence but, not having taken into account the deep ditch on the other side, he fell in an awkward position, was unable to rise and lay on the ground groaning with pain.

John saw what had happened and raced across to the aid of the horse, apprehensive for his safety. Not without reason, for when he reached Patch he saw that his right leg lay beneath him at an unnatural angle, like a matchstick bent in the middle.

'Only one thing to do!' muttered the farmer miserably. He stopped, rubbed the horse's neck, then unable to face the mute appeal in the injured animal's eyes, he rushed up to the house, caught up the gun behind the door, beside the crook, and went to do what had to be done before his nerve failed.

That same night he rode over to see the Huntmaster, and told him that he could not afford to lose a horse. The Huntmaster promised to bring the matter before the Hunt Committee as soon as it was possible to do so and with this the young farmer had to be content.

Chapter 13

SPENSER'S ARRIVAL

Once they knew of any loss sustained by a farmer through their activities, the hunt committee, in those days, were prompt in remedying the matter. They at once called upon their members to subscribe to a collection and the sum, brought along by the Huntmaster and the secretary, was paid to the aggrieved party in record time.

The goodwill of the farming community was valued by the hunting fraternity and farmers were glad to give their support for, not only were they thankful to be rid of a predator who preyed on their poultry, but they thought the English country-side a poorer place if the customs of centuries could not be maintained. They enjoyed the spectacle of the meet, took part in the chase for the sheer pleasure of it all and if they could not go on the back of a hunter or a humbler mount, they went on "Shank's pony".

No one had been a greater lover of the hunt than Joseph Yeoman. Only increasing age, and a growing stiffness of the joints after a variety of accidents in the field, had first diminished and then put a stop to his former exploits; but he never tired of telling and re-telling the stories of hunting episodes in which he had taken part, always expressing great pleasure in recounting who was present of the cream of society, and bathing in the glow of glory shed upon his communion with the aristocracy of the county.

'Many a time,' he would say with the shining face of one who had experienced the presence of God and his angels, 'I have ridden with Lord Willoughby and his four daughters,' and there was always one of those lovely maidens whom he favoured as having the best seat on a horse.

Knowing that his father could not bear to miss an opportunity for inspecting the parade of equine flesh at Cave's Repository for horses, when John received the money for the loss of Patch, he took Joseph with him to choose a replacement, not only to give the elderly farmer pleasure, but to benefit by his extra experience in judging the character, breeding and price of an animal that must fulfil more than one role on the farm and be strong enough to last for years.

There was, however, a second reason for the young farmer's desire for his father's advice.

A few weeks before Christmas that year a cold blast of early winter throughout the county had caused several accidents involving the slipping of horses on black ice, a treacherous condition of which drivers and coachmen had been insufficiently aware early enough to take the necessary precautions, and one of the casualties had been a treasured grey belonging to Charles Bennet.

With the winter still ahead the solicitor had decided to give the animal's strained muscles a full chance of recovery by resting him in the fields at Beauchamps, in the meantime replacing him with a new horse.

The coachman had notified the job-master and another grey had been brought round by the cob-boy immediately, but the new one was not a good match and Charles Bennet, who liked to keep up appearances, was dis-satisfied.

It was a matter of pride among the aristocracy and highly placed professional men of business at that time, to possess carriage horses which were perfectly paired and sometimes the agent, a dealer who specialised in the business, would search not only the country but the continent to find the animal required.

The solicitor had spoken to both his coachmen and his tenant about the matter, and had promised a good commission to the one who should succeed in getting hold of the closest match to take the place of the injured grey.

On the way to the Repository John broached the subject with his father, for he knew that Joseph had more contacts in this direction than he had the chance to make. The money such a deal could bring would make all the difference to the household finances at a time when it was badly strained, and with a new mouth soon to feed. He had said so to Victoria, only to see a small smile play around her lips and to hear her say quietly: 'No money ever comes to us as easy as that, my lad. You've got competition, so don't count your chickens before they're hatched!'

John came home that evening with a new half-legged horse for his own use and the next day tried out the warranty, testing the animal for faults that might have escaped his own or his father's keen eye, but the horse was strong, sound in wind and limb and those were the qualities that mattered. He was a good looking gelding from Holland with quiet ways and John called him Dutch.

A new grey mare, promised by the dealer approached at the Repository, came a week before Christmas. John tested out her warranty and as far as he could judge, found her without a blemish.

He drove over to the Harborne home of the solicitor with the horse tethered to the back of the trap and with Old Harry sitting there to keep an eye on her. The price was fixed at 105 guineas and instructions were given to the coachman to return the animal immediately after Christmas, the time allowed on the warranty, if found to be unsatisfactory.

It was on Christmas Eve that the coachman returned the mare and with a short statement that 'Master's not satisfied with this 'oss. Deals off,' he left again before John had time to enquire into the reason why. The Bennets were not coming over again until after the Christmas festivities were over, so John, feeling sore and dejected, kept the mare in the stable until he could take her back to the Repository.

The young Yeomans spent Christmas Day at Shortbridge and there, as a special supper treat, they sampled their first taste of tinned salmon, followed by tinned peached, for the canning industry had just been set up and the dishes were a novelty.

John waited until after supper before broaching the subject of the unsatisfactory grey mare. His father ruminated the matter in his mind like one of his own cows chewing the cud, then said: 'If that hoss is as sound as you say, there can be two reasons for the rejection. Either the coachman found an animal through another dealer and they got together to make a bigger rake off for themselves, or Bennet has a reason of his own and you won't know till you see him. Come to that, it could be both of those considerations. You'll just have to wait till you see him to get to the bottom of it.'

Five days later, the young Yeomans having returned home, an event of family importance took place at Beauchamps, when a smothering snowstorm hid the coming into the world of their second son.

John harnessed Daisy, the roan mare, to the high trap, set up the great green gig umbrella and battled through the silent whiteness to call the doctor and fetch the midwife. When the doctor at last arrived, covered from head to foot in snowflakes in spite of the shelter of his own gig umbrella, the midwife had already laid the baby near his mother and invited her to look at her new child.

Victoria turned wearily, and seeing an ugly, puckered face under a thatch of black hair, said in a shocked voice: 'Oh!' and turned her face to the wall.

Maybe it was this initial reaction that caused her second son to be the rebel he became, but for Victoria it must be said that she was not used to new-born babies having hair on their heads. Edmund had possessed none at such a time and he could do no wrong.

Edmund had remained a placid baby, which was looked upon as unusual in a first child. He had also gone on living, to Sarah's almost daily astonishment, for when he was not much more than a month old she had brought tears to his mother's eyes by pronouncing him too good to live long.

The Yeomans' first offspring had been named after a Saxon king because at that time John had become interested in the early history of the British race and the name of the kings of that period had caught his attention, so many of them beginning with the letter "E", which he found strange, and he wondered if there were some mystic meaning behind the initial.

It had been on one of the few warm days in late May during their second year at Cotewood, when they were sitting on the circular seat under the chestnut tree with its white candelabra lighting the spring green above them, that John read out the names to his wife as she sat sewing small garments for the expected baby: 'Edwin, Edgar, Edmund, Ethelred, Ethelbert, Ethelwulf, Egbert, Edward.'

When a son had arrived they looked up the meaning of "Edmund". Liking the sound of that one best, they discovered that it meant "happy protector of property" and thought it appropriate, for if he ever became a farmer, which they hoped he would, any property he might possess would certainly need protection of one kind or another and it would be good if he were happy in the process.

They decided that none of their children, and they hoped to have more, should have ordinary names since the family was already overweighted in that direction, with Thomases, Johns, Josephs, Williams and Georges. 'They shall follow your example,' remarked John to his wife, 'for you seem to be the only other Victoria in England besides the Queen and her daughter.'

During the autumn preceding the birth of their second son Roger Comptney had taken to coming down from his top storey flatlet to sit with the family by the log fire. On cold evenings it was warm in one of the chimney seats there and he was a great reader. In fact, ,such was his enjoyment of good literature he was often unable to keep the best to himself and would say to the others: 'Just listen to this!'

Then, in that deep, sonorous voice of his he would share with them some passage from a book just published. The most notable, but from their point of view the most sleep-invoking, was Disraeli's "Endymion", the

41

most humorous, Gilbert's "Pirates of Penzance", the most confusing, Dostoyevsky's "The Brothers Karamazov", and all these would generally be followed by discussion. The Yeomans were not academically minded as was Roger, but his enthusiasm and lucid explanations so awakened their interest that their minds opened like flowers under sunshine.

Over Christmas Roger had changed from prose to poetry, reading from Robert Browning's "Christmas Eve", knowing that Victoria would appreciate the likeness of the description to the scene of the little "chapel up the hill".

Then he read from "The Shepherd's Calendar" by Spenser, choosing the parts that he knew would appeal. Always the reading left deeper thoughts in their minds, and they were enchanted by the sound of the words, but when they discovered that the poet's Christian name was "Edmund" it seemed a portent. From that moment their second son had his Christian name — Spenser.

So Spenser Yeoman arrived to the fanfare, not of royalty as had Edmund, but of culture. He was born into an atmosphere when Shakespeare was read to his parents in the evenings that followed, and he was to become, years later, the most talented amateur actor in the village Shakespearean Society.

The moment his landlord arrived for the weekend in the New Year John "collared" him and with his usual forthright manner, asked: 'Why was the grey mare I sent you not to your liking?'

Bennet sensed that he was going to have to tread carefully. 'It was a capital match and I must congratulate you on that,' he replied, but my coachman got hold of another just as good. It was double the price so I thought about it, slept on it and decided that as a general rule one gets what one pays for. In other words your animal was so low a price that I was afraid it would turn out to be of low quality, developing later a fault that at present could not be seen.'

For a minute John was dumbfounded. The devious working of Bennet's mind in such a matter as this was beyond his understanding. It did not occur to him that although the solicitor knew a good deal about human nature, he knew next to nothing about animals, their quality or lack of it, and was obliged to rely on those who did know.

'That beast was tested out here and found to be sound in wind and limb and without blemish!' burst out the infuriated young farmer. 'Do you mean to tell me that you refused that mare because she was too low a price!'

Charles Bennet was used to dealing with people whose emotions got the better of them and remained calm.

'I am telling you a low price can mean a low grade,' he replied. 'You must also take into account that my coachman is an older man, has had animals passing through his hands for more years than you have and I was obliged to take that fact into consideration when I made my decision. The commission was open to both of you and one had to be the loser.'

What John would have said next his landlord never knew, for Victoria, who knew her man, knocked at the door, opened it and said: 'Excuse me, Mr. Bennet, but my husband is wanted outside in the yard, one of the ewes has lambed early.'

John turned on his heel and walked out in high dudgeon. In the kitchen Victoria laid her hand on his arm, saying: 'I heard you getting worked up in there and thought you'd better come out before you did any damage.'

John Yeoman threw her restraining hand off his arm, banged on the table, swore at the dog and said passionately: 'That "warock-sparrow"[1] of a coachman has taken that "tad-raddle"[2] for a ride!' And he rushed out of the house.

Sarah, who overheard that last invective, was shocked.

Victoria smiled. 'An educated man wouldn't know what any of that meant even if he heard it,' she said soothingly.

---

[1] "Warock-sparrow" — Bird of prey
[2] "Tad-raddle — Frog spawn

Chapter 14

COMINGS AND GOINGS

John Yeoman, having a great respect for William E. Gladstone, had been personally pleased when Disraeli was ousted from the position of Prime Minister to give way to Gladstone's second term of office, but Disraeli's death in April set every farmer in the district proclaiming in dogmatic and aggressive tones of voice, to anyone who would listen, exactly what he would do if he had the reins of government in his own hands.

It was as though, with the disappearance of that strong and colourful opposition leader, the balance of the State had been upset, and though the farmers might not have agreed with his policies neither must Gladstone have it all his own way.

If Roger Comptney happened to be in the yard when a neighbouring farmer, seedsman, carrier, buyer or seller dropped in on farm business, hearing what he took to be an animated discussion and liking nothing better himself than to exchange opinions, Roger began, at first, to join in.

He soon learnt to "hold his horses" however, for he found that these were not discussions but arguments in which reason proved to be no match against the aggressive dogmatism which the accountant deplored.

Listening without comment taught him that he had no right to denigrate, and in his desire to understand he came to see that the farmers' apparent arrogance was a defensive prop set up in a desperate attempt to sustain the uncertain structure of what had been, for centuries past, Britain's first industry. He also saw that he himself had no need of such self-administered support, for his life and work being steady and secure he was in no position to criticise.

John, as dogmatic as any other, was nevertheless making slow progress through the year 1881 after his second son had joined the household.

That winter had been severe and several people had lost their lives from exposure on Edghill, which had been his own birth place and his father's happy hunting ground. The Avon had been frozen over with skating from Barford to Warwick but in April the weather began to improve, crops followed suit, and though foot-and-mouth disease affected cattle on many farms and liver fluke still took toll of flocks of sheep here and there over the country, Beauchamps escaped these calamities.

On the twenty-fifth of June Joseph Yeoman came over to help with the cutting of the clover crop, and asked his son if he'd seen the comet pass over the night sky.

John replied that he had only seen the sky reflecting the lights of Bromsgrove Fair, to which his father answered, 'Ye've missed someat rare then, me lad, for it said in this morning's paper that it was the first time they've been able to take a photograph of one. Mind you,' he added, 'it didn't compare with Halley's comet. Remember it, lad? It was our first year at Shortbridge — 1859 it was — and I carried William out to see it. He were a bit heavy at six years old but he were dead asleep the minute before, an' I didn't want him to miss it. Mind you,' he repeated, 'I reckon that un that went over last night were a warning to them that are trying to rewrite the Good Book. "Re-vise" it, they call it. Ought not to tamper with the Scriptures, son, no good will come of that I'll tell ye.'

When harvest time came round and with it Joseph and his bagging hook, the papers were full of Gladstone's Irish Land Act, fixing tenures and establishing a Land Court to deal with rents.

'Eh,' remarked Joseph to his son, 'we have our troubles here with rents and landlords, but over there they have same, only twice as bad, so they say. It doesn't seem long since the Government sat on Ireland's backside for forty hours solid, trying to keep 'em in their place — during' that mild spell out o' season, remember? Back in February it must 'a been, an' they've been tellin' us to get off their backs ever since.'

'For as long as I can recall there's been trouble in Ireland,' said John.

'Aye, and as long as I can call to mind too,' answered Joseph. 'Remember the potato famine?'

'Too far back for me,' replied John, 'but what stays in mind is that the Irish are a fighting race and they've been standing up for themselves saying: "Our country right or wrong!" until it's become an everlasting motto with them.'

'Well, ye can't blame 'em, son, they've a lot o' wrongs to set right. Look at them absentee landlords, fer one thing, living it up themselves and charging rents up to the sky, taking it out of the farmers to pay fer it.'

'Aye,' said John, 'and I can feel for them. I reckon we've got a lot in common, them and me, we're always in trouble.'

'Well then, have someat else in common wi 'em,' suggested Joseph cheerfully, 'the fighting spirit that won't be sat on by yer circumstances. Any road ye got a good landlord now and look at that hayrick o' yourn standing good and steady, an' you ent had to borrow me rick tester this year.'

'Good, mebbe, but not plentiful,' was John's estimation. 'When the rick's good and twice the quantity I'll begin to think I'm making me way out of trouble.'

'Someone not good and steady, me lad, is that un over there,' Joseph pointed his hook at Old Harry who was working in a corner of the field. 'Come the winter and he'll like as not be laid up with the rheumatics. You need younger help than he will ever be able to give.'

'Low as they be, I can't afford to pay full wages, father.'

'Then get a youngster straight from school, you won't have to pay his wage till the year's up,' answered the elder Yeoman. 'Why don't ye go to Stratford Mop in the autumn, and hire a lad. Better still the Runaway Mop ten days later.'

'Then you run the risk of no one suitable being there, the possibility of an unsatisfactory lad and no time to remedy it. And where can I put him to sleep? I can't turn the old folk out, for there'd only be the Workhouse for them to go to.'

In the orchard Amelia Yeoman was helping her daughter-in-law to sort early fallen apples that were to be peeled and made into chutney for the market, and there a similar conversation was taking place over Sarah's creeping age and decrepitude.

With Edmund now two years old and Spenser eight months, with the increasing work brought into the house by the slow but steady increase in the farm stock, more milk so more butter making, more eggs to be collected from poultry, the cooking for the lodgers, the processing, preparing, storing and packing, the increased washing and cleaning, not to mention the everlasting need to make something out of all the odds and ends, there was never any time for anything but work; Sarah and Harry Dock daily became more of a liability than a help. It was impossible to keep pace with all that had to be done.

When they had been young Sarah and Harry had brought into the world six children, three having died in infancy. Of the remaining three, one, being an excellent shepherd, was sent for by a farmer who had emigrated to Australia. The other two, a son and daughter, were married with families that filled their small cottages to overflowing, so that there was no room for another human being.

Sarah and Harry had never had enough money to save for a cottage of their own, and those fortunate to have their own roof over their heads and a family to help them to keep it there, spoke with fear of the Poor House, and with pity for those within its walls. Even those who could look forward to a future secure from the thought that they might end their days there, used the fear of it to keep their children from idle ways. 'If I don't work hard,' an industrious father would tell his children, 'I might end up in the Workhouse and so might you!'

From the time of Henry VIII the State had made attempts to cope with two problems, treating them as one. Poverty and vagrancy were given the same solutions right down to the building of the present nineteenth century institutions. For the State the problem had never been an easy one, but there had been times in the past when the treatment, meant to discourage malingering, idleness and taking advantage of the parish help, had degenerated to downright brutality and the senseless degradation of the victim who seemed unable to help himself; for amongst the bevy of afflicted were deaf-mutes, mentally deficient, the blind and the handicapped of every kind, and all were treated in the same way.

Old couples coming late to the workhouse were separated on arrival, and this action alone was responsible for the hopelessness amongst those forced to end their days there, while pains were taken to make them all feel that they were an insupportable burden on the parish providing them with shelter.

Shelter and food, both of the lowest order in some cases, were virtually all that was given. With the exception of a New Year's party, neither comforts of any kind nor human sympathy and understanding were ever included in the curriculum, because these were regarded not only as unnecessary, but out of place and irrelevant to the situation.

It was no wonder that Sarah and Harry would not allow the thought of it to enter their minds, for they knew that the fact that they had worked hard all their lives would be of no account in such an establishment.

The harvest that year went on too long for the corn to be good. The last week of August saw heavy rain which brought wide-spread mildew and the wheat began to sprout even as it stood stooked in the field. In the beginning of September, however, a good drying wind sprang up and at last the harvest, such as it was, was carried. The root crops were excellent.

As autumn drew on the two old servants grew stiffer in the joints and John turned to Victoria and said, 'What shall we do?'

His wife answered, 'You must go to Stratford Mop and I must call at the "cottage up the hill".

Chapter 15

MOPS

On Sunday Victoria started out earlier than usual for the chapel "up the hill" with the two children in the wicker pram.

As she drew near the cottage where Ivy lived she slowed down, pushed the bassinet to the front door and knocked. When Ivy, surprised at the early hour, slowly opened the door, the farmer's wife asked, 'May I see your mother, my dear?'

'I'll fetch her, missus,' Ivy answered, looking curiously at Victoria, for this was the first time such a request had been made..

Ivy's mother was a hard working, rather blowsy but cheerful woman. Her husband brought in about eleven shillings a week as a farm labourer; even with the extra wages earned at harvest time and potato picking it was not enough to support a large family, so his wife left the younger children in the care of the older ones when they came home from school, while she went out to do odd cleaning jobs and to collect the washing which she took in daily. With Ivy at home on Sundays she gave a hand up at the "Big House", and it was just as she was getting ready to set out that Ivy announced, 'Mam, it's the lidy from Beauchamps.'

When she heard the reason for the visit she beamed and said in an even broader Brummagem dialect than her daughter, 'There naaow! And there was Oi a-wondering where to send her fer her first job in service! Her's just left school and Oi had a mind to send her fer a hinterview at the "Big 'Ouse", but the old housekeeper there's a tartar and no mistake. Fer her first place her needs someun a bit on the unnerstanding side, if ye gets me meaning. And as fer going away and living-in sommer else, she croise her oise aaout every toime Oi says a word abaaout it.'

'Well now, when could she start?' Victoria asked.

'Whenever ye want her to come, Mrs. Yeoman, barring today, if ye'll excuse her. Her as to look after the little uns while Oi'm up at the "Big 'Ouse" on a Sunday, but her can come fust thing tomorrow and welcome. Did ye want her to sleep in, or dily?'

'Daily, please,' answered Victoria. 'That's why I particularly wanted Ivy, because at present we have no room to sleep another in the house.'

'Well Oi doan't mind telling you, Mrs. Yeoman, ma'am, Oi wernt look forrard to her going to some stranger who moight be good to her or moight not; Oi be moighty glad her be a-comin to you. Oi been a-telling her how, in moy day, the young gals went to the Hiring Mop and stood in a loine loike a lot of hosses, woil the lidies who wanted a gal to work fer 'em looked 'em up and down to see if they be strong and healthy, and that's how Oi come to get me own fust job; but ye don't see much of that now.'

The farmer's wife took a shilling-piece from the green crocheted purse that hung round her neck, reached for Ivy's right hand and pressing the coin into it, clinched the bargain with a gentle handshake.

'There now,' said the girl's mother, highly delighted. 'Ye're in ye fust job, me gal, ye're oired now fer the year. Ye must go round fust thing in the morning.'

Victoria, leaving the bassinet as usual, went on up the hill with Edmund trotting beside her, Spenser on her arm, and a small smile playing around her mouth. She was pleased.

****

Ivy had been working at the farm for some time when John set out at Michaelmas for Stratford Mop to find a lad for the farm work.

He started off early with the mare and trap in order to reach the town in good time to look round and leave again before the roughs from "Brum" began to drift into the town. They would have their own good time getting drunk and picking fights with the bands of gypsies, when it needed no more than one of the booths to be over-turned to start a riot.

'And mind your money, the pick-pockets'll be about,' called Victoria. She had been before and the noise and crowds did not appeal to her so she was staying at home.

John took Harry Dock with him, realising that it might be the last time the old man would be able to enjoy anything like it.

The Stratford Mop was the seond largest fair in England. It had begun as a Hiring Market around the middle of the fourteenth century when a law required every able-bodied man to hire himself at a fixed wage in order to meet the shortage of agricultural labour caused by the Black Death in the reign of Edward III.

Labourers were hired by the year, from Michaelmas to Michaelmas, and the transaction was sealed by the payment of the Hiring Penny (which over the period had become a shilling piece) accompanied by a shake of the hand as a sign of good faith.

"Runaway Mops" were held ten to fourteen days later to give the chance of resolving unsatisfactory conditions on one side or the other, though often this did not work out as was intended, for the runaway servant, if found, was taken back and given rough treatment as punishment.

Young women had, in the past, joined the line of labourers, carrying pails and mops, just as the cowman, shepherd and wagoner each carried their own badge of trade: cow's tail hairs, fleece or crook, and whip.

Girls and women were no longer seen in the market, but men and lads still proferred their labour in spite of the determined efforts of the body of concerned men who did not approve of humans offered for sale like so many cattle. For small farmers who had little cash to spare it was a service of which they still made use, and they saw no harm in it.

Well before they arrived in the town the two men could hear the sound of the steam organ grinding out its own particular brand of mechanical music. As they took the mare out of the shafts and left her with the trap at a farm John knew of just outside the town, they could hear the shouts of those who were sliding pell mell down on the Big Mat, while high aloft they could see the turning of the Big Wheel.

In the town itself the noise was deafening, but John, glancing sideways at Harry, saw that he was enjoying the sights, and the noise seemed not to worry him.

They walked round the side-shows, viewing the Fat Lady and the mummified Siamese twins who died young; admiring the Strong Man who could lift fifteen hundred weights on his back; squinting at the peepshows, trying their luck at the shooting gallery where John won a prize; and both shied at coconuts until they gained one each, for this was a "must" to take home to their wives. They watched the children laughing as they tossed up and down on the mechanical sailing boats of the feature "Sea on Land"; then both were caught up in a small crowd regarding with deep fascination the actions of the Fire-eater.

Here and there among the milling crowd they caught sight of a cowman, a wagoner or a shepherd each with their distinguishing mark. In smaller market towns with hiring mops these men would be standing in a line, but here they mixed with the throng, while those requiring their services kept their eyes open until they saw what they wanted. Then conversation took place, and if both were satisfied the bargain was struck.

But John had set his eyes on no odd-boy when they wandered over to the Agricultural Hall to see the show birds. There were fine poultry breeds, pigeons ('Oi dunna wanna see any o' they dratted birds' was Old Harry's remark here), singing canaries (Oi, wunna moind one o' them, though'), and the colourful foreign breeds — parrots, macaws, cockatoos and lovebirds; after which there were the oriental Java sparrows, the Spice bird and the black-headed manakin to wonder at.

They stopped to look at the skeps of bees; especially at one beehive of glass through which they could see the activities of the industrious creatures at work among the combs.

They saw a variety of rabbits ('Oi could do wi' one o' them fer me supper tonight' Old Harry murmured) but the only kind that really interested them were the long-haired white angoras, with a lady sitting beside them spinning lengthy strands of the wool taken from their bodies.

They returned to the milling throng, making their way to Bridge Street to be sure of their slices of roasted ox meat, the speciality of the fair day. On their way they passed groups of folk standing round rails that kept them clear of the fires over which pigs were being roasted on spits in the adjacent streets.

It was at this point that the two men lost each other in the crowds through which they jostled their way towards the ox-roasting. They met again at the far end of the trestle table which had been set up in Bridge Street to serve those waiting with covered dishes to take the meat hot to their homes for the midday meal. There, with newspapers in their hands, the farmer and his man received their own portions, and it was while they were eating the delicious slices of joint that Harry nudged his master's arm and jerked his head in the direction of the pavement near the spit.

Standing there with a wistful expression on the pale, rather vacant face was a weedy looking lad of about thirteen or fourteen years, and in his ragged coat fixed at each buttonhole in turn was a dirty piece of sheep's wool, a snatch of hair from a cow's tail, and the longer strands of black horse hair, while in his hand there hung the broken top of a shepherd's crook.

'He's a measly looking gawkin, but mebbe he's better'n he looks,' was Harry's side-remark. 'To go be wot he's decorated isself up with, he's a odd-boy a-waitin' for a maister, though he looks keener on that grub there than on a hiring.'

John looked at the lad for a moment, then decided that even if the lad were no use to him, at least he could buy him a meal for he looked in sore need of one. He pushed his way through the crowd to the boy's side.

'Looking for a job as odd-boy?' he asked casually.

'Aye,' said the lad, without at first taking his eyes off the slicing of the meat at the table. Then he realised what had been asked of him and glanced warily at his questioner; but his eyes reverted quickly to the food as if it were all-important to him at that moment.

When his chance came John bought a portion and gave it to him. The lad could scarcely believe that he was holding meat in his hands with a piece of John's newspaper enfolding it, and gazed at it as if it were gold. Then he guzzled it as though he were half-starved and could not wait to get it down.

'What's your name and where do you come from, lad?'

The boy gave the farmer a long hard look before he answered. Then apparently satisfied with what he saw, added to what had happened, he replied in somewhat surly tones. 'Me name's John Brown, an ar cum fro' Broddy.'

'Were you in a job at Broadway or were you born there?'

'Were born there,' said the boy shortly. He hesitated, gave John another searching look that had a hint of cunning in it, opened his mouth as though to speak, then changed his mind and closed it.

By this time Harry had worked his way over to John's side and while the boy turned his attention to the remaining crumbs of meat in the newspaper, Harry said: 'He's loike an 'oss wot's bin badly broken in. He's not trusting ye yet. Had a bad maister and run away's moy guess.'

John knew there were lads who stayed nearly the length of the hiring period and that there were farmers who, during the last few weeks before the year was up, treated their odd-boys so badly that they ran away, thus relieving the farmer of the necessity to pay them the £3. 10s for the twelve months' hire. These farmers then went to the next mop, hired a new boy, and the same process was repeated so that the employer never had the expense of the odd-boy's work.

'Had a good master in your last job?' was John's direct enquiry.

'Nay. He fed me on sop morning, noon and night, and vera near starved ar were,' the boy burst out, before he had time to be careful what he was saying. 'Said ar were no good to un, and beat me wi' this yare strop. Ar snatched it out on his hand and bruk it in two, and ar run away wi' it.'

Harry nudged John again. 'Mebbe he's a bit on the simple side, but med be a wukka. I've known 'em loike faithful animals if they loikes ye, and he wudna 'av told ye all that if he didna loike the looks of ye.'

So it was that John returned home with his odd-boy on a year's hire. Also, from the farm where the mare and trap had been left, he bought some geese for his wife, for Victoria had said that a farm was not a farm unless there were geese there, and this gift was to be his proffered statement that Beauchamps from nothing had become a farm.

Victoria was happy about the geese, understanding her husband's meaning by the gift. But she was doubtful about the odd-boy. Little did she know that he was to be with them all their and his working life.

Chapter 16

"THE SPIKE"

The advents of the enthusiastic Ivy and the simple minded John Brown, now called by everyone "Young Jack", were lightening the work both inside and out, when a sudden, though not wholly unexpected turn-about took place in the shape of two exeunts and one entrance effected in quick succession.

Harvest had been gathered in after drying winds at the end of August saved it from the mildew and sprouting which had been the bane of the previous summer. It was stacked good and high, drying in the draught that blew through the air holes of the big barn. The constant, unending struggle of the tenants to bring the farm on to a steadier basis after its violently rocking start was having effect, and one of the agents in achieving it was that hitherto "fickle jade", the Weather.

This year it had at last returned to a more normal routine: winterly from January to March then a fair summer on and off. May had been marred by a thunderstorm when lightening had rent a tree in Alvechurch from top to base, and at the same time the village clock had ceased to work because of a fractured pendulum and a minute hand that had mysteriously disappeared.

One morning in September Victoria was up early with the twenty month old Spenser, who had been inconsiderate enough to vomit on awakening, apparently for no particular reason since he was perfectly all right again immediately after being cleaned up. He and his three year old brother were dressed, their mother wondering all the while why Old Harry did not bring hot water to the door at the usual time.

Sarah was not in the kitchen when the farmer's wife took the children downstairs. The fire was unlighted, and the kettle cold.

The children were settled at their breakfast as speedily as possible, the fire lighted and the kettle put on to boil while Victoria listened anxiously for movements in the room above. She was sure something was amiss when Old Harry stumped down the stairs, opened the door at the bottom and said in a puzzled voice: 'Oi canna waken th'old 'ooman, missus, and its usually her as wakes Oi.'

Victoria climbed the steep steps, noted the unusual disarray in the room and went quickly over to Sarah's bed. She saw at once that the old woman would never wake again. Sarah Dock had finished clumping down the stairs, her work was done and she had gone to her rest.

After that Old Harry "went downhill". He could not recover from the loss of his life's partner. He was unable to wake in the morning, he could not manage the stairs to bed without help and when he reached the great flock mattress it was to throw himself down without undressing.

In the daytime he would look at the job that the farmer had given him to do and be it in cowshed, yard or stable, there he was an hour later sitting on whatever came handy, staring into space and muttering to himself.

John was concerned because Victoria was, at any moment, expecting the arrival of their third child and he was afraid she might have Old Harry ill on her hands when she could least do anything for him.

There was only one thing left to be done and though it was hard to bring themselves to the decision, they were obliged, in the end, to send the old labourer to the Workhouse.

Victoria, feeling guilty, comforted herself that some improvements had taken place that year at the dreaded pauper-house which vagrants nicknamed "The Spike".

On the Board of Guardians mainly responsible for the over-all organisation and conditions of the poor-house sat the respected elders of the neighbourhood, all of whom were deeply conscious of one fact: that if they spent too much in the way of improvements there would immediately be a public outcry over the increase in rates.

It was a hard fact borne in upon their minds so continually that even when they had any desire to improve the lot of the unfortunates under their care, they were hamstrung by such a never-ending obstacle.

This particular year a new member had been elected who, besides being a younger man with a fresher outlook, was not content with what he learnt from the fortnightly meetings but went to see for himself what conditions were like.

During the bitter weather of the previous winter he had, on several occasions while passing on his way to work, seen the long, pitiful queues of widows, blind old men and lame old women standing in all weathers, rain, hail, snow and biting winds along-side the building where they were to receive the pittance which literally stood between them and starvation. Having walked sometimes as much as four miles, there they stood from eleven o'clock in the morning until three, four or even five o'clock in the afternoon, having been too late on arrival to take advantage of the doubtful shelter of the stone-cold corridor inside the building.

There they waited while the Board, sitting in a warm room, debated the merits of each case. Some went home to children that they had been obliged to leave all day, regardless of illness, either their own or their children's. Others went home never to recover from the effects of the long wait.

As a result of proposals put forward by the new member (who asked forgiveness for his youth) a new system was established, which did something, though not enough, to alleviate these hardships.

As for the residential side of the matter, after continual pleas from the examining doctor who visited the inmates, the matter of food was looked into, and some improvement took place in this direction also, but it mainly affected the children. One of the members of the Board was so far moved as to make the remark that some prisons had better diet and catering than this institution.

A new building had been planned but, due to a legal conflict between Board and architect, nearly a year had passed and there was still no signs of building taking place.

Old Harry went dumbly, no longer caring, into the old men's ward, where in spite of the efforts made by the staff to keep the place clean and tidy for the inspection of the visiting Committee, there was always the stench of incontinence, an odour which kept away other well-intentioned visitors who were unable to endure it for long.

Victoria was too near her time to visit the old man but she spoke to Ivy about it, and the girl persuaded her mother to spare an hour or two to go with John in the trap.

Harry Dock had taken to his bed and hardly knew who was visiting him. His fingers continually clutched and crumpled the rough sheet and when John spoke to him he stared blankly, unknowing, and unconscious of the general air of hopelessness into which his fellow ward-mates had sunk.

Ivy's mother shuddered and they left, never to see him again, for he died a few days later when typhoid fever broke out in the institution.

Then, on a day when a strong westerly gale brought much of the orchard fruit still left on the trees thudding to the ground, Victoria gave birth to their daughter.

The child was named Madeline, for no other reason than that, just as Victoria seemed to be the only one of that name in England besides the two in the royal family, so to their knowledge, there was no other Madeline in the realm, and according to her father, no other child like her, for he idolised her from the start.

Chapter 17

THE NEW-COMERS

'So John Brown's dead!' was the cryptic remark uttered by Roger Comptney as he came through the kitchen from the yard to his rooms, one evening in 1883.

'What!' exclaimed John and Victoria in one breath. 'But I can hear him putting Sheikh away now!'

'No, no, not that John Brown,' laughed Roger, 'the servant that bossed the Queen about for so long. That old Scotsman she thought so much of. And what will she do without him now she has fallen down the stairs and brought on an attack of rheumatism? He won't be there to push her chair about for her.'

'It never rains but it pours,' remarked John. 'It isn't long since that assasination attempt on her life, and I hear that The Grand Old Man is so worn out that he's had to go abroad to get away from everything for a while.'

'Well, no wonder! He's passed his three score year and ten by about three years, hasn't he?' questioned Victoria, and she went on 'And I reckon the Queen wouldn't be sorry if he stayed abroad for good, she likes him so little.'

'Oh, he won't do that yet,' was Roger's parting remark as he passed on into the passage, 'he's determined to try and solve the Irish Problem after giving them the first electric trams and a couple of years to think whether or not they want Home Rule as well. I reckon that'd solve the problem for us anyway.'

Mrs. Bennet greeted Roger as she passed him and came to call Victoria into the sitting room.

'Look at this, my dear,' she said to the farmer's wife, 'what do you think of it?' She indicated the dress she was wearing.

'What a beautiful silk!' exclaimed Victoria, touching the material with a delicate gesture.

'Ah, but that's where you are wrong,' smiled the landlord's wife, 'it's the first artificial silk that's been manufactured. Don't you think it's an excellent imitation? And what do you think? I had it sent from London by the new parcel post that's just been started!'

'There's always something new coming along these days,' exclaimed Victoria again. 'I really don't know what Old Sarah would have said!'

'She would have looked at my dress and said: 'Oh - ah, missus, but ye niver know wot's agoin' to 'appen to all these new-fangled contraptions. Us'll 'ave te wite an' see, wunt us? Supposin' it falls to pieces around ye, then wot'd ye say? An' as fer all this yere gas and 'lectrics — Oi 'eard as they turns ye green!'

The two women laughed over the old servant's ways. But she would have proved right in this case, all the same. There were problems, and artificial silk was not to come to the general public for some years.

As for turning people green, the newly competing gas and electric companies kept their light-giving properties to the towns, and the word "green" took on other meanings as the old industry of farming itself was receiving something novel. Conservative minds and the "fickle jade" were going to see to it that it would be a long time before such new-fangled ways were accepted. There were too many who thought the same way as old Sarah.

It came about that same year that the Midland Farmer's Club, in its attempts to cope with a problem even more long-standing than the Irish question, was clapping its collective hands. It thought the answer had been found to the annual difficulty of haymaking under soaking rain that never let up long enough for the long swathes of grass lying in wet fields to dry off.

The Club explained and demonstrated silage, a new process whereby grass could be cut wet, carried wet and stored wet all quite satisfactorily.

But the Weather was not to be out-witted in this fashion! It smiled to itself at man's everlasting arrogance, and proceeded forthwith to make silage irrelevant at once by producing the best summer known for years; at the same time it created a neat new problem for the farmers: how to find enough harvesters to gather in the abundant crops!

Victoria was happier than she had been since her wedding day. And John was singing in the fields!

She blessed the brass tap in the kitchen which gave them a never-failing supply of cool spring water throughout the hot summer, when the supply below the floor dried up and the pump outside the back door showed signs of a "go-slow" action.

The new baby was content either in the old wicker cradle or in the bassinet which had so faithfully served both her brothers.

She delighted her father when he sat her on his lap at breakfast time and gave her dunked hot toast in strong sweet tea, for it was clear by her waving hands mutely asking for more that she shared his chief table preferences.

The little room with a window looking out on the passage at the bottom of the stairs now served as nursery where Edmund and Spenser spent a great deal of time playing, while Madeline, in all weathers, was put out in the bassinet under the cedar if wet, out in the orchard if fine.

Often, as she lay and watched the chasing shadows and the waving branches of the fruit trees, a pale young face would insert itself between the hood top and the green leaves of the tree above. As she was in the habit of smiling up at all faces irrespective of to whom they belonged, she smiled at this one too, though here a process was seen to be in reverse, for usually she would smile in response to one which beamed down on her, here the pale young face would slowly melt in response to hers.

The odd-boy never touched the child in the bassinet until the day when the farmer's wife, coming through the gate into the orchard, saw John Brown stooping over the baby with a grin on his face. She stopped in wonder for a smile had never been seen there at any time before this. She stood at the gate and watched.

He stayed there for a while, just looking and grinning with a hesitant kind of happiness, as though he were puzzled by a new emotion which had never found a way into that dim spirit before. Then, as if satisfied, he waved his hand at the child, again in response to Madeline's own action, and he went off whistling tunelessly.

Victoria said nothing but kept her eyes open. After she had seen the same thing happen three or four times she stepped forward and taking no notice of Jack's guilty start she picked up the baby and put her in the starlted lad's arms.

He looked at her from the dark shadowed eyes with mouth open, the grin gone.

It was then that Madeline gurgled with pleasure and laughed up at him. He looked down at her and slowly the response came again to his own face. He rocked her gently as he had seen her father do, then he looked up again at his mistress, so small a figure, no taller than he and for the first time he smiled at her, a crooked twisting of the mouth.

He gave the child back to her, waved his hand and went off whistling no recognisable tune.

There was no doubt about it that Young Jack was dull-witted. Ivy, round-faced, red cheeked and quick-witted, said; 'Eh, missus, he's nine-to-the-dozen, in the top storey but he fair loves the babby, and he'll be good to them two boys till them're old enough to start taking the mickey out on him.'

When Sarah died Ivy more than took her place. A healthy, bouncing girl with blue eyes and fairish frowzy hair, she took home a shilling a week in wages, the recognised amount for a "skivvy" in her first placing.

She came first thing in the morning before the household was down and did as Sarah had done. She lit the fire and took up hot water. Then, while the young mother attended to the baby's needs, she dressed the boys and left them in the nursery until she had cooked the breakfast, at which everyone sat down together.

She had all her meals at the farm, going home last thing at night simply to sleep, and she had half a day off once a fortnight. Her mother gave her back threepence out of her wages which she was free to spend or save as she wished and she was happy in her first experience of independence.

She sang about her work whether it was emptying the slops or scrubbing the floor without soap (Victoria had ruled out soap for the floor at present, as an unnecessary luxury which she could not yet afford). She took the children for walks, learnt quickly, came to know Victoria's ways of doing things and did the same willingly, halving the work of the house for her mistress.

For the farmer it was a different matter.

Young Jack did not learn quickly, but with patient handling and a repeated showing of how a job should be done he grasped the idea then repeated it on his own until it became a habit. He was able to handle the horses, harness them, and take off the tackle and hang it in its proper place on the wall. Anything that was a set skill requiring repetition without alteration he could master as long as there was no thinking attached to the task. A change of tactics because of some individuality in the needs of the animals was beyond his comprehension, and could sometimes mean an unexpected fracas in stable or cowshed from some animal not receiving its specialised attention.

He slept in the "glory hole", a small compartment under the back stairs just large enough for a bed, and he was no trouble except for occasional fits that set him trembling from head to foot, finally bringing him to the ground groaning and writhing. The doctor, when consulted, was of the opinion that if these were epileptic fits they were mild ones, probably due to some accident when minor brain damage had occurred during some period in childhood. They were nothing to be concerned about and he might grow out of them in time, while the fact that one leg was shorter than the other almost passed without notice.

The boy's pale face and dark sunken eyes aroused Victoria's pity and John's protective instinct. Careful questioning after one of his fits brought the information that: 'Ar were knocked down be a runaway 'oss and cart and ar were yurt in th'yead and tuk to th'orspickle. Arter that me yead didna yurt but ar cuddna 'member fings.' Enquiry about his family brought only vague answers in which they learnt that he had "budders an' sesters" but of his parents they could learn nothing.

The task he most liked of all the odd jobs he was given to do was that of collecting wood for the fires and this he would do whether there was any need for it or not, and regardless of the weather, an element which he totally disregarded.

He would come in sometimes soaked to the skin, and as he had at first only one suit to wear, he sat and shivered in his wet clothes until the farmer's wife, afraid of pneumonia, would take him and strip him by force, for small though he was, she was stronger than the weedy boy who seemed never to have been properly nourished.

He was given one of John's old night-shirts until his clothes were dry, and this he kept in the glory hole for him 'to put on at nights' Victoria patiently explained, though she was doubtful whether he ever did this until the second time he came in dripping wet.

This time she called Ivy to fill up the hip-bath for her while she divested the shivering lad of his sodden clothes.

The bath was placed in front of the fire and filled with hot water from the kettles and pots. He was told to get in and wash himself from top to toe and left to get on with it by means of a bar of yellow soap left on the flagstones by the bath.

When John came in to see how he was getting on, the lad was sitting in the water-filled bath, clothed in the night-shirt and fast asleep as he leaned against the tall back.

In the farmyard his vagaries could be a nuisance and there were times when John lost his patience and swore at the odd-boy (swearing for John was usually 'Dang ye, lad!').

On these occasions Jack's already pinched face would turn grey and he would retire to the saddle room where he would sit completely immobile, unresponsive to any calls to 'come and get on with it.' In the end the farmer always had to go for his wife, the only one who could pacify the lad and get him moving again.

Because of the odd-boy's limitations John was obliged to decide whether to get rid of him at the next mop or to keep him and have another labourer who would be experienced and reliable. He could do with a man and a boy but the purse strings were still pulled tight over more air than cash. He discussed the matter with his wife and she had the solution.

Ivy had mentioned the death of a neighbouring farmer with the farm passing into other hands. There was a young man there, an experienced cowman and wagoner who wanted to change his place of employment. He lived only a quarter of a mile away at the corner of the Roman lane. Victoria asked Ivy to get in touch with him and to ask him to come up and see John.

In the meantime she drove over to see her father in Shropshire.

Neither of her parents had ever come to visit them either at Cotewood or Beauchamps since the wedding five years ago, and there had been no communication between them apart from a gift of money each Christmas from Victoria's parents to her.

Victoria's father was a rich wool stapler owning a coal mine, and property in the city, and neither he nor her mother had approved of the marriage of their daughter to a handsome young farmer who had no money.

Their off-spring however, possessed a determination of spirit which was out of keeping with her small figure and quiet personality and nothing they said or did altered her intention to marry the man of her choice.

Her mother had seen to it that she had a splendid wedding, thus adding to John's already strong feeling of inferiority; then she had washed her hands of the whole affair.

Victoria's father had said: 'Well, we'll have to make the best of a bad job. I suppose without that fellow's sheep, wool staplers would be in a poor way!' He settled a dowry on his daughter that would not come to her until she reached the age of twenty-five, which would be next year.

When she reached her old home she asked her father if she could have part of her dowry in advance. He asked the reason, then said; 'What did I tell you!' All the same she went back to Beauchamps with enough money to pay the year's wages for a labourer. The good summer was to set the balance right but that had not come along as yet.

So it was that Billy Six-Foot came to work at Beauchamps after the death of Old Harry. His real name was William Saunders, the youngest of a large family now grown-up and out at service. One brother worked at the brickyards, another in the tanyard, a third was wheelright for the area and a sister was a barmaid at "The Fox and Hounds" on Weatheroak Hill. Billy was very tall, hence his nick-name, ugly but full of good nature. He was twenty-one years old and a willing worker who became John's "right-hand", as much a treasure on the farm as Ivy was to the farmer's wife.

Chapter 18

MANURES

Between Beauchamps and Shortbridge, until this year, there had been sufficient help available within the circle of family and friends to cope with the poor crops and harvests due to the continuing bad weather. This year the abundance of crops in both districts meant that neither of the members of the family had time to travel the six miles between farms to exchange aid and, as was the custom between farmers, it was the nearer neighbours who combined forces, borrowing and lending labour, tools and themselves, first on the one farm and then on the other; Hubert English came with his labourers to help John Yeoman and the latter went to Rough Green Farm in return.

Neither of the two farms could afford to buy the machines that the more prosperous farmers were introducing into the work of harvesting. 'Any road I like the old scythe,' said John, 'it cuts cleaner and closer to the ground.' 'Oh, ah,' rejoined Hubert English, 'there's nothing more satisfying than the swinging of the knife as it cuts through the swathes and lays them low.'

'By gad, your clover crop's good,' said John, staring at his neighbour's lush fields. 'I've never seen any as good anywhere. What manure did you use, farmyard muck, saltpetre or guano?'

'Basic slag from steelworks.'

'What!' exclaimed Yeoman, 'I've never heard of that used anywhere.'

'I've been trying it out for a year or two and found it never failed to increase the yield, and with this year's sun, well, you can see the result.'

Work had gone on well into the evening, Mary English taking the men their tea in the hayfield, and when John Yeoman arrived back at the farmyard he met Roger, riding out on Sheikh for a horse-back journey round the sweet-scented, new-mown fields in the cool of the evening.

'Well, and what d'ye think created those sweet-scented fields in the first place?' John asked the accountant.

'Farmyard muck, I shouldn't wonder.'

'Not a bit of it.' And John, meaning that literally, told him the news of the new fertiliser.

'Well, I know nothing of that sort of thing,' replied Roger, 'but if you'd asked me I'd have thought it would have burnt the ground bare instead of producing a field of honey-filled flowers. But what's this guano you mentioned?'

'Sea-bird manure collected from islands off South America,' John informed him, 'and I can tell you one ton of that stuff is equal to thirty tons of farmyard muck.'

'Good stuff then!' Roger was again surprised. 'Long way to come though.'

'Ah, and with such a small area of supply the day will come when there's none left. Good thing something new comes along to take its place.'

'Well man, I reckon that's the way of life.'

The summer weather went on until the corn crops were gathered in that year, with harvest supper held at Rough Green Farm. Among the usual helpers entitled to sit down to it were a gang of Irish labourers. They had come over from their troubled island to make a quick turn-over of cash at the different harvests and were staying on to deal with the potato and root crops.

It was after these celebrations were over that, with evenings drawing in again, Roger Comptney as was his habit in the lamp-lit hours, came down into the sitting room and sat in the chimney corner with his book.

'Olive Shreiner's "Story of an African Farm",' he told the Yeomans, 'fascinating. Want to hear a bit?' And of course they liked it so much that it became a serial reading.

When they were about a quarter of the way through Roger ceased reading one evening, turned to his listeners and said, 'Enough of this for a while. I want to ask you something. Have you heard of the "Penny Readings" that are all the fashion in town pubs and village halls, and in all sorts of places?'

'No,' answered the farmer and his wife together.

'Well, just as I am reading to you here, it appears that there are many readers who are doing just this, not to two listeners only, but to a roomful at a time. I've been thinking about it.'

He paused a moment, then went on: 'There's little enough to entertain the people around here. The nearest "Penny Readings" are at Redditch. What do you think about the idea of starting a centre here?'

His listeners were silent, considering the proposal.

'There's another point to it,' Roger resumed. 'Children are spending longer at school and learning more than their parents know. They will have a larger knowledge and a wider outlook, a good thing in its way and leads to progress, but it can become a divisive influence in a family. Now Penny Readings can be a family affair. It would give older and younger something to share and talk about together. And John,' Roger made a direct appeal at this point, 'you remember telling me about fertilisers?'

'Manures. Yes.'

'These readings could turn out to be mental manure spread on the fields of the mind. Who knows what good crops would follow with Joseph Arch a-ploughing the soil of their thoughts with his politics.'

'Oh-ah!' said John, bring out an objection. 'I'm not that sure as it's a good thing to make labourers think. If farm hands get educated they won't want to stay on the land, they'll be off for better money when they've got better brains and then where shall we be? I can't do all the work on my own.'

'I doubt if what I have in mind will make all that difference along that direction,' replied Roger, 'but it will give them something to lift up their minds *while* they work, and that's what I want. I have no intention of educating them away from you. Besides, it's not only the labourers I want, but the farmers and their wives and children, anyone who would like to come.'

'What is it you propose to do?' asked Victoria.

'Readings from famous works of poetry, prose and drama: Tennyson, Thackeray, Shakespeare, Dickens.' The accountant rolled off the names of the great like ribbon off a reel.

He appealed to John again, in a different vein. 'And you John, shall delight them with your folk-songs and rounds, with Billy Six-Foot to sing with you, just as I have heard you both in the fields. And that's a delight in itself after a day's work as I come home in the evenings.'

'You've a good voice yourself,' put in Victoria. She turned to her husband. 'John, we could give it a try. If it doesn't catch on we can give it up straight away.'

The news spread quickly. Labourers took the message home with them; neighbours passed it over the hedge; to the local shop and public house and it was given out in the notices on Sunday at chapel.

On the first Sunday in October the big sitting-room was prepared. The long oak refectory table was moved with great difficulty into the kitchen. Chairs and stools, anything on which a seat could be taken, were brought in from all over the house. Then, to Victoria's great delight, Roger Comptney installed a second-hand harmonium he had bought at a sale of household goods in a town auction.

The children, wondering what it was all about, were taken up to bed earlier than usual.

Then, at six-thirty that evening, farm workers lit the way up the path for their families with their lanterns held before them and, entering red-faced and bashful, took their places.

Floats and traps drew up and disgorged the neighbouring farmers and their wives and children, and the white iron gate squealed out its welcome to each new-comer.

To set them at their ease Victoria played an air on the harmonium which they all knew:

'Come lasses and lads get leave of your Dads,
    And away to the Maypole hie...'

What did it matter that it was not the Maypole season! They all knew it, boots began to tap the rhythm on the floor, and with Roger's fine voice leading, voices at first shy and low gathered volume and the ceiling began to shake with:

'Willy has got his Jill, Johnny has got his Joan
So trip it, trip it, trip it, trip it up and down!'

And of course, what could be expected! The loud rhythmic beat pulsed over the log fire and up the chimney, rousing four year old Edmund and two year old Spenser from their beds.

They crept in their night attire through the little half-size door into their parents' room, over the cold oak floor and down the stairs to sit at the bottom, listening to the strange sounds coming from the other side of the sitting room door, looking at each other wide-eyed and wondering. They knew the tune, joined in with their childish trebles but missed the sequence and carried on singing after the last verse was finished by the assembled audience within.

Those nearest the door heard, guessed and began to smile broadly, passing the message along to their mother. If Victoria had counted on this happening she could not have hit on a better note of making all feel at home!

Ivy made her way through the gathering to the door, took them by the hand and led them into the room. Someone made room for them to sit, one on Ivy's lap, one on their mother's in the warm chimney corner, where they stared at the people lit by the lanterns hanging from the blackened ceiling beams.

Victoria began to sing softly to them:
'We are but little children weak,
Nor born of any high estate...'
and in a moment the children who went to the little "chapel up the hill" were joining in, and a second later, to everyone's surprise the tenor voices of the young Irish labourers were heard, for it happened to be a hymn they knew from their own childhood in Ireland, the words written by an Irish woman, the music composed in Dublin.

The faces of the two small children were filled with wonder, and Edmund, laughing with delight, sang the first verse after they had all finished, at which the whole company applauded and the ice was well and truly broken.

Roger, who had intended next to recite Edgar Allan Poe's dramatic poem "The Bells", decided that neither that nor the following item prepared, "The Charge of the Light Brigade" which was to have been rendered by Charles Bennet, was suitable for the little ones and instead he took from his pocket some notes he had made from a local newspaper which had offered material for just such an occasion. It was a sermonette on the subject of "Old Mother Hubbard":

'She was not young but on the other hand she could not have been old enough to have been a grandmother, or the rhyme would have read: "Old Grandmother Hubbard", but there were no children there so they must all have grown up and left home. She could not have been bed-ridden or she would not have got to the cupboard and but for the dog she was alone, so she was very likely a widow. It was a poor home or the lines would have read: "she went to one of the cupboards" but no, my friend, there was only one cupboard. She was a *very* poor woman.

'Her dog was as poor as she was, he must have been half-starved. If she only expected to find *one* bone, there must have been several with which she had made her last meal of bone soup. "But when she got there..." It took her some time to reach the cupboard so, friends, can you picture the poor old soul, full of rheumatics, slowly making her way across the room, and when she got there it was all to no purpose. There was nothing there either for herself or the dog. I appeal to you, my friends, what sort of husband must she have had to leave her as poor as this?'

Roger paused for a minute before bringing his final points home. He gazed around the room at the upturned faces all alive with interest in this familiar figure they found they had never really known before. Then he resumed: 'The lessons to be learnt, my dear friends, are four: One — to avoid being a widow. Two — not to marry the kind of man Hubbard must have been. Three — to have more than one cupboard. Four — don't keep dogs that want bones.

The accountant had maintained a straight and solemn face over all these pronouncements and watching the faces of his audience he had seen the shock of absurdity over the first exhortation, the surprise of the second, the struggle to smother laughter over the third, and the final inability to restrain irrespressible laughter after the fourth.

The members of the audience turned and looked at one another and bursting into gusts of mirth, the tears rolled down their cheeks as they rocked in their seats at the humour that had taken them unawares. The children caught only the last point and laughed because the rest of the company did.

After this the women cried and the men loudly blew their noses over a poem. It was about a rich man who had no children and was offering a large sum of money to a poor family who had seven — if they would only let him take one of theirs. The audience followed in imagination as the needy parents went round their sleeping children in an effort to decide, eventually concluding that they were unable to part with a single one of them for any promise of future secuirty.

The poem was read with pathos by the solicitor, to whom Roger had passed this more suitable material entitled 'Parental Love''. After all, they could give the parents the stronger meat later. They had started where the audience was, not where the instigator of the idea was, thought Roger to himself.

During the recital of parental love triumphant in face of great difficulties, the children fell asleep and were carried back to their beds without awakening.

On their way back as they descended the stairs, Victoria said to Ivy, 'Well, the children know all about it now, maybe they'll settle to bed next time without any trouble.'

'Oh,' said Ivy, the practical elder child of a large family, 'I'd let 'em come in fer the fust part, an' let 'em go off to sleep like tonight, nobody 'ud mind, them 'ud all unnerstand, an' it sets the visitors at ease 'an all.

Downstairs there was a complete change of mood as John and Billy Six-Foot sang jolly rounds, inviting everyone to join in with them as they pealed forth "Hark! the bonny Christchurch bells" and "Great Tom is cast" followed by "Let's have a peal!" and laughter was mixed in with the singing of "My Dame hath a lame tame crane!"

By this time they were all ready for the lemonade drinks brought in by Ivy, and everyone streamed out into the night not in awkward shyness but in enthusiastic enjoyment, still singing "Come follow, follow, follow..." and as they made their separate ways home the general feeling was expressed by the words uttered along the lanes, 'Gor! but that was good, eh! Hasn't So-and-so missed summat! I bet un'll come next time.'

Throughout the winter those fortnightly Readings proved the mental fertiliser Roger had intended. It fed the community spirit, bringing the seed that was to flower in the fulness of time in the shape of the best amateur performances of Shakespeare's plays that any village community might produce. And curiously enough nearly a century later, with the "Penny Readings" long forgotten, there was to be a repetition of them one evening, a little different in form, under another name, but in essence the same to be enjoyed by the children and grandchildren of those who climbed out of bed to come and listen in 1883.

Chapter 19

JACK GOES HUNTING

Every week-day and Saturday morning it was the odd-boy's first task to bring Sheikh from pasture or stable, harness and gear him to the gig and have him ready tethered at the gate for Comptney's drive to the station.

By November this was taking place by the light of the stable lamps and one morning in 1884, as the accountant came out of the house to set off for his journey to work he saw, as he did most days, the dim figure of the cowman bringing in the buckets of frothing milk from the cowhouse after the early morning milking.

On this occasion, after the usual cheery greeting always exchanged between the land labourer and the city worker, Roger stopped to talk to Billy Six-Foot while Young Jack held the horse for him.

'Well, my lad, you've got the vote now. What do you intend to do with it?'

'Got a what?' asked the cowman, with as much astonishment as if he had been told he had a baby.

'Why, I said you have a vote. When the next general election comes your opinion as to who should be in the Government will be as important as mine.'

'Eh! Will it now, sir?' exclaimed Billy in much the same tone as before.

Roger pressed the point home. 'We can only give one vote, lad. Come now, what do you mean to do with yours?'

'Woy, sir, Oi 'adna give it a thought!'

By this time the accountant had mounted his seat in the gig and, holding the reins still for a minute, he continued his lecture to the unthinking labourer, his mind going back four years to the day when he first came to Beauchamps and talked to Harry Dock on this very subject.

'Well, Billy, I shall not tell you, nor must you let anyone else tell you for whom you should vote. But I want you to think about it, read the papers and talk about it, then make up your own mind what to do about it. Now I must be off or I shall miss the train.'

He gave a jerk on the reins and the gig moved smartly out of the yard leaving Billy standing there looking after him, with his good-natured mouth wide open and the buckets of milk dangling from the yoke on his shoulders.

During the conversation the odd-boy had been leaning against the wall listening. He watched the cowman slowly turn to take in the milk, then he said, 'Wot were you two inkle-weaver's chatter-nagging abaht then, Billy, eh? Wot's that fing, a vort, eh?'

He opened the kitchen door for the six-footer to go through.

Billy stooped under the door, took the buckets through the dairy, came back into the kitchen, stretched himself to his full height, scratched his thick poll of tousled hair and said slowly, 'Eh, young Jack me lad, blowed if Oi can tell ye. Moind, Oi'v heard the men at ''The Fox and

Hounds" a-blowin' their tops off abeout that there vort, but Oi niver tuk that much notice afore, Oi were too busy on the Shove-ha'penny.'

'What's all that about then?' asked John, who was at the table eating breakfast.

Billy recounted the lantern-lit conversation in the yard and John explained the meaning of the mysterious commodity called the "vote", advising him much as Roger had done.

'Then,' suggested the farmer 'be the time the election comes round you might know sommat about it.' He pulled his boots on and added: 'On the other hand ye might not!'

He turned to Billy as he stood up and the cowman noticed that the farmer was not in his ordinary working clothes.

'I'm out today, lad, so you're in charge. And Jack, you take Dutch up on Hill Field and harrow the ploughed land there.'

Yeoman went out to saddle the roan mare as Hubert English came into the yard on horse-back, and a few minutes later they rode away together.

'Another excellent harvest, John,' remarked English.

'So good I reckon we'll never see better,' was John's rejoinder.

'Never known the crops so early and good with it.'

'Trouble is the drop in prices after a succession of bad years. Seems like ye've got to keep running to stay in the same place!' John's tone was lugubrious.

'Oh, ah, but never mind John, a good harvest two years running is enough to put heart into a man again.' Thus the two men talked as they rode towards the meet at "The Fox and Hounds"; and soon talking changed to singing and that at the tops of their voices.

Young Jack was too late arriving at the top end of Hill Fields to see his master riding with his friend along the old Roman trackway.

The hill showed signs of once having been an ancient fortification, for Jack had to drive Dutch up and over and round three separate lines of banked and ditched defences, which had been so worn down by the centuries that only a vestige of what had once been there remained for those who could read the signs. On the eastern side no earthwork revealed itself as the meadows swept down to the lane which had once been a sizeable Roman built road, double and treble the width it was now, after farmers of long years had each taken a portion of it to add to their fields.

With ploughing Young Jack was capable only of acting as lead-boy to the horses, but harrowing was something he could manage by himself, and never was an odd-boy prouder than when Victoria gave him lunch to take with him and a job of work he was trusted to do on his own. His pale face glowed with pride and the whole day would be spent doing it thoroughly — as a rule.

On this particular day no one guessed that anything untoward was going to happen as Young Jack moved up and down the upturned soil under the November sun.

From earliest childhood the odd-boy had known the Hunt. He had grown up with its periodic appearance in the country lanes and fields and like most country folk he had been fascinated by the sound and sight of it. Whenever the scarlet and black, and the tan and white apeared he ceased whatever he was about, as did most of the spectators around him, to watch the colourful cavalcade go by; and no one then thought of questioning the morality of such an event either in the watching or in the participation of the sport. Its activities went back over the centuries to the time when man asserted his hardly won domination over the animal world, his quarry then being at least six times his own size and his survival depending upon his ability to outwit his opponent. Over the centuries no one regarded the shrinking size of the quarry and the reversal of roles, the trapping of the little by the big. The fox, however, was still a predator which depleted the stock a farmer could ill afford to lose.

None of these considerations entered the mind of Young Jack as he drove Dutch over the ground and whistled tunelessly; nor did they concern him when suddenly his eye was caught by the well-known colours moving to and fro in the distance beneath the waving arms of a windmill on a hill. The riders were assembling outside the local inn that morning and the odd-boy's eyes were drawn like a magnet to the bright scene.

He manoeuvred the horse into a better position on the hill-side and watched as the huntsmen moved off with the pack. Within minutes the hounds had their noses to the grounds as they sought the elusive scent in a nearby field.

Absorbed in watching, Jack dropped the reins. Dutch, looking round, noted that the driver had his mind on other matters, and taking advantage of this fact, slowly, unobtrusively, moving over the furrows to the grass at the hedge-side, he began to munch, turning the whites of his eyes to see if the driver had noticed his wily action.

Suddenly one of the hounds gave tongue, there was a shout, the horn blew and everything began to move at speed.

It was irresistible.

Without a glance at the cunning animal seeking his own bit of pleasure, Jack left Dutch to his own devices, sped down the fields and over the Roman lane, pushed through the hedge and scrambled up the opposite slope.

He as fleet of foot, light and thin. Three years of good food, fresh air and contentment with his lot had made him as healthy as he would ever be, and now a new light shone in his eyes.

He could not see what he was following but he pursued the sound of the hounds as they lifted their voices at the top of the ridge. He could hear the thudding of the galloping hooves and feel their vibrations through the ground beneath his feet. He followed the hunt by ear, on foot, and he was gone for the day.

John Yeoman was with the "Field" but both he and Hubert English were too absorbed in staying with the hounds to see the slight figure topping the rise and running across the fields behind them.

Young Jack himself was too intent on the trail to identify his master among the galloping crowd of followers. His eyes were on the pack, for wherever they went he knew the fox would be somewhere there in front.

And if any of the mounted followers caught sight of Jack for a moment they were too used to seeing foot travellers to notice anything more than that there was always one at the back of them.

* * * * * * * * *

When John arrived back at the farm in the dusk of the early evening, Billy Six-Foot, just finishing his day's work, asked an unexpected question.

'Have ye seen that young Jack anywheres, Master?'

As Billy took the mare, unsaddled, unbridled and rubbed her down, he went on after John's negative reply. 'That young scaramouch, he ain't bin back all day. Oi bin up on Hill Fields, and there was Dutch munching grass by the hedgeside, dragging the harrow arter him, and be the way them furrers be a-worn down round the edges Oi reckon Jack's bin gone most of the day.'

'H'm. He's never done this before. Well, all right Billy, you go home, I'll see to that Jack of ours. If I need you I'll ride over for you.'

He went in for his meal and heard the story again, first from his wife as she took the eldest of the three children to bed, and next from Ivy, who had just put the two youngest to bed and was on her way out.

After supper, tired though he was, the farmer took a stable lantern and searched Hill Fields again, but in vain. It was as he stood gazing down towards Weatheroak Hill and saw the winking lights in the windows and yards of "The Fox and Hounds" that the thought entered his mind that Jack must have seen the Meet from where he was harrowing. Could it be possible that he had followed the hunt?

When Jack did not return at his usual time for bed both Victoria and John became uneasy.

Victoria lit a small lamp and left it in the kitchen window, placing a plate of food on the table. The doors were never locked either at night or at any other time.

Both the farmer and his wife, equally exhausted after the day's differing activities, fell sound asleep.

In the morning they came downstairs to find Jack's supper still on the table untouched. There was no sign of him either in the "glory hole" or in the saddle-room, where in summer he often slept on a sack filled with straw, a retreat of his own choosing.

Then Ivy, a little late, arrived breathless and excited, with a strange story to tell.

'Hey, Master, Missus, ye won't find Jack anywhere around here, but I can tell ye where he is!'

Master and Missus looked at her in some trepidation.

'He's in a police cell!'

The now buxom girl put her hands on her hips and let out peal after peal of laughter, not only at the sight of the two faces looking at her in such astonishment, but at the news she had to impart.

Victoria, somewhat sharply, asked the reason for this incarceration saying that she considered it hardly a matter for laughter.

Ivy pulled herself together and went on:

'Well ye see I heard the tale on the way here from Reuben, cowman at the English's, as he walked down the road with me. Seems Reuben were at the "Stag" in Redditch last night when Young Jack went there with a thirst that made him a bit bold like.

'He gave them the sound of the hounds giving tongue, and it was so good that each of them farmers treated the lad to a half pinter ale and then got him to do the "View Holloa" afterwards. And that were good and all, so Reuben says, so they each give him another draughter ale and he up and give 'em the 'orn as well.'

Victoria and John listened to all this in silence, both women proceeding with the work to be done at that time, and John putting on his boots in readiness for whatever action was required at the end of Ivy's recital.

Ivy resumed in her own blowsy, vivacious style, punctuating her sentences with a hearty chuckle at the picture she was presenting to her listeners.

'Well I can tell ye, be the time he'd had payment in ale for all his tricks, Reuben says, and I believe him, fer that lad's never had a lot of booze afore, ye could have lifted up an arm and pumped beer out of him like water out of that pump by the back door there!' She paused to take breath, then took up the tale again:

'Any road, at closing time he were turned out, still hollering, and he went through the town and down Mount Pleasant giving the 'ounds, the "View Holloa" and th'orn at the top of his voice, until he'd woke up all the babbies in the road.'

She laughed again. 'Reuben says the women were a-grumbling to their men, as they come home from the pubs, that the Yunt was a-going through the town at near midnight!' She went off into another peal of laughter, then finished off the drama:

'Th'end of it all was a bobby on duty picked him up, took him to the station and charged him wi' being drunk and disturbing the peace! He were put in a cell cryin fer ye to come and take him home, and Reuben says as far as he knows he's there yet!'

John looked at Victoria. She said, 'Finish your breakfast first and then go for him. If he's waited this long he can wait a bit longer, and perhaps it will teach him a lesson.'

When the farmer arrived at the police station he found a boy to hold the mare and look after the trap, then he strode in to find Jack.

He explained to the sergeant on duty the mentality of the lad and asked him to be lenient with him.

The sergeant took John to the cell, informing him that the fellow had cried all night, continually pleading to be let out. When they reached the cell Jack was still crying and moaning over and over again, 'Let ar out. Let ar out.'

When he saw John he was overjoyed, a great grin spread over his tear-stained face and he said, 'Ye've come at last, maister, at last ye've come! Now they'll let ar go, wunt 'em?'

He was released without being charged. John took him home and had a word in his wife's ear, not to do too much scolding.

Young Jack told her, 'Ar be never a-goin' to set foot in that there tun agin. Ar'll be a-goin nuntin agin, ar loikes it foine, but niver through no tun no more!'

The story went the round of the hunting circles through Hubert English, who heard it all from his cowman, Reuben. And there came the day when Young Jack went hunting again.

After his next spree across country he arrived back in the farmyard a remarkable sight. It was dark there, and Billy had gone home so that no one saw him until he limped into the lamp-lit kitchen where the farmer and his wife were finishing their supper with Ivy, the children all being in bed and asleep.

Completely exhausted having run and walked for miles, he collapsed on the settle without a word and lay there full length, his eyelids fell and sleep overcame him at once.

At first the others did not recognise him. Thinking they had a whipper-in, suffering from an accident on their hands, they jumped up and went over to him in great concern.

On closer inspection they all exclaimed: 'It's our Jack!'

He was dressed in the clothes of a hunt servant with a red coat, pair of breeches, black hunting cap on his head and riding boots on his thin legs. His pale face was white with fatigue, his sunken eyes closed in sleep, but his lips were curved in a beatific smile, as one who had reached heaven.

Victoria sat down heavily and with the Welsh blood of her ancestors surging in her veins she said, 'Well! Goodness gracious me, deed to goodness now! Who'd have believed it?'

Ivy clapped her hands to her mouth to stifle the rising mirth while John, looking more closely, said, 'Someone has given him these. They are old. Look at that darn in the jacket and the patch in the breeches, and the boots are well scratched under the polish.'

So it turned out.

A whipper-in at the kennels had recently received a new outfit and having heard about the new devotee of the hunt, had taken him on one side; after a word with him he had taken him indoors, divested him of his old clothes, which he threw on the fire, and dressed him there and then in the new ones — his own discarded outfit.

From that day forward Young Jack never wore anything but someone's worn-out hunting togs, and he was never known as "Young Jack again. His name became known throughout the county as "Huntsman Jack".

Chapter 20

A SHOCKING CRIME

Throughout the Penny Reading season in 1884 the gathering audiences at Beauchamps had topics to discuss which kept their tongues wagging while they found their seats and sat waiting for their homely entertainment to begin.

'Hey! Wotyer think now? They've found a new pain-killer, an wotyer think it is? Nobbut cocoa!'

'Cocoa! Ye daft 'a'porth ! Ye mean cocaine!'

'And wotabeout the new trains runing through a tunnel under Lunnon! Them Lunnoners wanna watcheout! Them'll find 'emselves dropping through a crack one of these days on to one of them trains and being carried to goodness knows where!'

'Oh, ah, t'ent safe to go up te Lunnon. Oi reckon th'ole city'll fall through a chasm and the poor folk in the train'll find 'emselves buried alive afore they rightly knows where they be!'

'Well, there's one good thing. The Gov'ment's having a good look at bad houses at last, and abeout time too!'

'Oh, ah. Ye could find yerself buried alive in some of them back-to-backs in Brum afore ye rightly knows where ye are. Oi ought to know, with a sister living in one.'

'Eh! but wotyer think of the Duke of Wellington's funeral? Oi 'eard as how he were buried in three coffins. D'ye think he were that big he wuddna fit in to the ordinary large size un, ad had to be cut up into three pieces!'

'Eh, now, Oi reckon they musta left him a bit too long afore they nailed im up and had to use another, but oh, by gor! Three, d'ye say?'

'Oh, ah, and then them three were covered all over with a blood red velvet pall.'

'That'd be for style, not use, after three coffins. Nothin could get through *three*!'

But all these momentous national events counted as mere trifles compared to what happened one dark night early the following year in the very roadway down which some of them travelled by lantern light to Beauchamps.

It was one February evening when Billy Six-Foot went home by moonlight, ate the supper his mother had ready for him and made his way the few yards up the road to "The Fox and Hounds" for his usual game of Shove-halfpenny.

Outside the door he met Tom Branch, a bankrupted farmer turned roadman. The old man had been filling in pot holes worn in the road by winter frosts and wagon wheels and was going inside to "wet his whistle" before returning home to his small cottage up the hill in Rowney Green hamlet.

While the two men were drinking a pint of ale together a somewhat wizened figure entered, pushed past a group of men at the bar and, ordering a tankard of ale for himself, brought out of his pocket a small box from which he took a pinch of snuff that he applied to his nostrils as he waited to be served.

Under his worn out old overcoat collar his neck and chin were swathed in a red and black knitted scarf to keep out the night cold. The sleeves of the coat were soiled with red earth, as were his trousers, and the boots were as old as the coat. They were covered with red clay mud and through the cracks in the uppers could be seen a hint of dirty white stockings.

Beneath his arm was a carelessly rolled old striped pillow tick and slung over his arm a frail, the reed basket used by workmen to accommodate their lunch and other articles for the day's work.

'Eh, man,' said one of the group who stood at the bar, looking askance at the mud on the snuff-taker's clothes, 'You'm a-poaching rabbits that's plain to see. And wot next? Someun's chickens, Oi'll be bound.'

'You mind yer own business,' answered Aaron Crabtree, sourly.

'It'll be our own business if you come sneaking arter any of our honest hens tonight,' put in a second man.

'Eh, and ye'd better take care now an' all,' warned Alvechurch Charlie, who lived in the church belfry. 'There's a new young constable come on the beat around here since you were last about these parts. Had me up for being drunk and disorderly a wik or two back, and Oi do know as he's dead keen to kitch ye since he heard tell of you and your ways.'

'Shut that gob of yourn.' Aaron let out an oath. 'Oi tellye it'd take two bobby peelers, both on 'em young, strong and hearty to kitch me, me lads. Oi got me wits about me.'

'Oh, ah, and there *be* two bobbies round about here, both with their wits about 'em and if they was to meet up with each other jist as you come along in the dead of night with that bag of yours full of dead birds, then ye'd be for it and no mistake, neither!'

'Not bloody likely,' answered the unsavoury old fellow, blowing his nose on a foul handkerchief. 'Oi bin about these parts on and off long enough to be wise to their ways, and Oi knows all their meeting up places and one of 'em ent my tent.'

'Eh, stop ye gostering,' requested the first man, turning away.

'He's nought but an ole buffer, but he's crafty as an ole dog fox,' remarked Tom Branch to Billy Six-Foot. 'Looks like one too, come to think on it,' he added, with a glance at Crabtree.

He rose from his seat ready to leave. All his farming life he had made it his habit to retire early to bed in order to rise early, and though no longer farming, his old habits held. That was not his present reason for leaving, however. He had a sensitive nose which could not endure the rank odour of the poacher, nor his bragging dirty mouth.

'He's noght but an ole rip-sky!' he said in an undertone to Billy, as he made his way out. 'And Oi'm not a-staying to hear no more gab from the likes of he. Moight see ye on ye way to work in the morning, Billy. Got a few 'oles to fill in along the Roman road, an' ye know me. Oi loike to be at it early like.'

Billy stayed on for his game of Shove-halfpenny, and half-way through he looked up to see the poacher leaving for his night's work. When the game was finished he yawned and turned to leave.

'Yo be roight early bird like ole Branch,' called out Alvechurch Charlie.

'Oh, ah. An' Oi'm not so fond o' me guzzle an' wazzle (food and drink) as wot ye be!' Billy chaffed him.

Alvechurch Charlie was in the habit of drinking too much, and to sober himself down again would run all the way home to the church belfry. On his way through the square he would plunge his head in the cold water of the village horse trough or, if it were frozen, under a neighbouring pump.

As Billy made his way out, the new constable about whom Aaron Crabtree had been warned came in and went over to the bar. The tall labourer caught the landlord's first words, 'Crabtree's back in the area. Has his tent pitched in that track half-way along the Roman lane, usual place.'

'Bit cold fer a tent this time of the year, ent it?' remarked the officer of the law.

'Eh, he's a tough bird, that one. He knows how to kip himself warm all right. That's why he's just bin in here. He only has his tent for headquarters and that's where he'll go now to have forty winks, no more, then he'll git his work done when everyone else is asleep. You could see he'd set his gins aready, when he come in here. Then he'll off to the early market to sell whatever he's been able to nab, and back home again afore anyone knows he's bin away.'

The next morning Billy Six-Foot set off to work, lantern in hand, for the February mornings were dark as night. It was not long before the young labourer saw a light in the distance that wavered and gleamed along the Roman way.

'That'll be ole Branch. He said as how he'd happen be along the lane this marning,' he said to himself, and began to whistle a tune.

When he caught up with the roadman he was surprised to see him sitting upon his barrow, his lantern held forward over the road in front of him.

Billy looked down to see what it was that the old man was regarding so intently and with such a strained expression on his face. In the circle of light he saw something that made him catch his breath, then expel it with such force that it came out in a whistled 'Phew!' an expression so inadequate for what he was feeling that he added another equally bankrupt exclamation: 'Lawks a-mussy!'

Lying there on the ground at the feet of the old roadman was the new young constable, his uniform slashed and muddy, his helmet gone, his face white with the pallor death.

'Is 'e - is 'e dead?' stammered the cowman, in a daze of astonishment. In the dim gleam of the lantern he saw the dark sticky flow of blood into the reservoir that already lay in a pool on the rutted road.

Branch did not answer. He was a figure turned to stone, his lantern still held out at arm's length as though that limb was a branch growing out of a tree, with the lantern a gigantic luminous leaf trembling on the end of it, shaken by the wind of the emotion within him.

For a moment the two men remained motionless, gazing at the horror on the ground, helpless in their bewilderment.

An owl hooted in the trees on the rise and its dark shape flew across the first glimmer of dawn. The unearthly sound matched the scene and awoke the men from the trance into which both had fallen.

The roadman put the lantern down on the barrow beside him, and it was he who spoke first, 'Billy, you better go quick to Beauchamps. Tell the gaffer someone must go to the police station in Redditch.'

The cowman looked up and nodded slowly. He was still held in the spell of an experience beyond his reckoning and made no move.

'Git on with ye then, William!' said Branch sharply. 'No good a-standing there.'

The owl hooted again in the trees beside the way and Billy looked up to see daylight growing in the eastern sky. It made him think of milking time. He was late for it and it was this thought that galvanised him into action.

'Oh, ah, Tom,' he said, his words coming in a series of staccato jerks. "Oi'll go, Tom. But fer a minute me legs wouldna move noways. Eh! Wot a goin' on! Wot a goin' on!'

He ran all the way to the farm taking a short cut through the fields and burst into the silent kitchen hoping to see Ivy, who had not yet arrived.

He stood for a moment in the quiet house scratching his head in perplexity and wondering what he should do.

In the room above one of the children awoke and paddled about the floor and at the same instant he heard Ivy coming up the path. He opened the door for her and she stopped in surprise at the unprecedented action. Billy opened his mouth to speak. For the second time words failed him at the thought of the enormity of the happening in the lane. He stood there his eyes wide and staring, tongue-tied, inarticulate with shock.

'Wot's up, lad?' asked Ivy, seeing the consternation on his face. His tongue was loosened. In a short time she had the picture before her mind's eye.

Ivy was a practical young woman, used to crises. She went straight up to the Yeoman's room and called John out. John shouted down for Billy and got the story from him.

'The cows will have to wait,' the farmer said decisively. 'Take the mare and trap and get into Redditch as quick as you can, Billy. Get someone from the police station to come out with you.' Then he went to Roger's room before going back to tell his wife what had happened.

Before long the whole family was down in the kitchen. The farmer and his wife, carrying hot sweet tea in a can wrapped in flannel, went along to the lane to see if there was anything they could do. After all there might still be life in the victim of the attack.

Jack was roused and told to be quick and harness Sheikh, and the accountant set off early to call at the doctor's house in Alvechurch before catching his morning train.

When John and Victoria reached the spot where the roadman still sat on his barrow watching over the dead policeman they gazed down in horror, but they could see at a glance there was nothing they could do for the young constable.

The farmer's wife had brought brandy substitute, a brew of her own recipe made up at the chemist's shop and containing a restorative with no alcoholic content, which she firmly believed was better than the real thing. She had intended it for the constable had he proved still to be alive, but she gave it now to Tom Branch for she saw that he was cold and shivering with shock.

'Take this, Tom' she encouraged him, 'it'll do you good. Then we'll all have some hot tea and we'll feel the better for it.' She turned to her husband.

'You go back and get the milking out of the way for they may need to use the house later on, and there'll be a busy day ahead. I'll stay with Tom here until the police arrive.'

John looked at his wife. There was a frown of anxiety on the normally calm face but she was as composed as ever. He could not help wondering at the boundless store of inner tranquility she possessed, no matter what happened. She was so small, her strength so great.

Then he went without a word to do the cowman's chores, an ordinary task on a day out of joint.

Chapter 21

JUSTICE IS SEEN TO BE DONE

Travelling as fast as the mare could carry them, William Saunders, accompanied by a constable, drove back to Rowney Green from Redditch and on the way he gave the police officer information as to how he came to be involved in the scene in the lane.

When they reached the spot where old Branch sat waiting for them they found that the doctor had already arrived and was completing his examination.

The physician stood up, straightened his back and said, 'Stab wounds on the body seem to have been inflicted by a weapon such as a clasp knife. And by the way, Mrs. Yeoman was here keeping Branch company. No place for a woman, this. I sent her back to the farm.'

For a moment the officer of the law made no reply.

He stood looking down on a colleage with whom, only a few hours previously, he had kept company on the night patrol of the parish borders. They had parted to walk their appointed beats, and now - they had parted for good.

He turned to Billy Six-Foot. 'Well Saunders, you've your work to do, you've done your part here. Better get back to the farm. Let's have those things out of the trap first, though.'

When the cowman had left the scene the constable turned to the doctor and said, 'What time did you say that death took place?'

'Between two and four o'clock in the morning, I would say.'

'Any weapon found?'

'Only the constable's own staff. Found it underneath the body when I turned him over,' was the doctor's answer. He continued: 'Sorry to have done my work before you arrived, but from the message I received it seemed there might be life in the man, and life's more important than procedure.'

'Right, doctor. Now you've your surgery and patients to attend to, and I doubt you've had your breakfast yet. I'll carry on here.'

As the physician departed in his own gig, the constable looked round the area immediately surrounding the body.

There were so many foot-prints woven and interwoven with the comings and goings of the last few hours it was going to be difficult to pick out any one particular set to which extra significance could be attached. Besides the patterned mesh of many feet in the mud of the trodden path there was a patch at the road-side where the ground was churned as if indicating some kind of struggle, and here there seemed to be only two sets of footprints.

He got Branch to help him place posts in the ground, and the area was wired off with the requisites he had brought along with him in the Beauchamps trap.

He questioned the old man while they worked and having made notes on the answers he left the roadman on guard until his own reinforcements arrived from Redheath.

Walking along the lane he came to the track leading off to the left where the poacher's tent still stood. The only things to be found there were the straw-filled sack on which Crabtree had taken his "forty winks" and the tarpaulin sheet with which he covered himself. The man himself was nowhere to be found. After interviewing the landlord at "The Fox and Hounds" the police officer possessed information which gave him a good idea where to look for the poacher.

When Aaron Crabtree was apprehended that same night he was found in one of the back-to-back houses of the poorer quarters of Birmingham. The sleeve of his coat was soaking in a bucket of water and on the wash-stand was a clasp knife which had been washed and wiped clean, though there was still mud on the handle, and when it was later examined traces of blood were found in the joint.

Blood tests were not so efficient then as they are now, and the difficulty which could not be resolved was whether the blood found on the knife, the sleeve of the coat, and on other items belonging to Crabtree, was that of a human or that of an animal he might have poached.

The evidence needed to establish Aaron Crabtree's involvement in the crime would have to be stronger. And there was one odd article which could not be found. It was the frail which the poacher was carrying when he entered the inn on the evening previous to the fateful events.

The suspected man was examined by the doctor for a wound on the head.

'How did you get that?' A pause. Then the sullen answer came. 'I fell against a lamp-post when I was drunk.'

'When did that happen?' Another pause, then, 'The week before last.' The doctor himself paused before he went on to say, 'That wound has been inflicted during the last twenty-four hours.'

In an excited voice bordering on hysteria the poacher answered, 'I tell you it was not. I should know what happened to me own head! I was drunk, I tell ye, and the lamp-post was in me way.'

'That wound is consistent with a blow by a policeman's staff!' Aaron Crabtree let out an oath and spat on the ground. 'Never, I tell ye. Never, damn ye!'

At "The Fox and Hounds" for the next few weeks there was an unusual animation in the buzz of conversation which centred exclusively on the deed that had been done in this quiet country place, where anything which excited interest and offered a fresh topic for discussion rarely rose beyond the normal rural occupations and relaxations. Quarrels between neighbours, an unwanted baby's arrival, an early death by accident, an occasional wonder at a freak of nature either in the elemental, animal or human realm, all of these had occurred before. But never this — never murder! It was certainly beneficial for the landlord's trade! The male inhabitants of all the cottages for miles around were busy gathering at the inn.

With some folk imagination ran riot, but others, bearing in mind the newspaper reports, were more sensible in their speculations as to what had happened in the dead of the night when the secret contest took place between two men, one a habitual though mild breaker of the law, the other a keen enforcer of order, the latter becoming the victim in the full strength of his youth, the former a killer with ebbing powers and small physical energy.

The enlarged group of men around the bar debated the matter between them. The facts were not all gathered; there was as yet no proof that the man arrested was a murderer; everything was still at "the alleged" stage; there had been no trial, but here the outcome was already pre-judged. Here everyone knew WHO had done the deed, they were now busy on working out HOW it was done.

'Oh, ah, old Aaron was a crafty old buffer, no doubt about it, but whoever woulda thought he'd go as fer as murder, eh? was the general question that expressed everyone's feeling about it.

'Well, Oi looks at it loike this: it'd have hurt his proide loike, if he was caught arter all that gostering (boasting) t'other noight,' was one idea put forward.

'Eh, landlord, wot d'*yo* think happened 'atween 'em, then?'

The landlord answered slowly, weighing his words carefully. He had been warned by the constable who questioned him not to discuss the matter, but his position there left him open to temptation.

'Well,' he said, 'I reckon —' The struggle between duty and desire damned the flow of words for an instant.

'Aaaah, aye, and wot then?' asked one, impatient at the pause.

'I reckon that, after patrolling the border with his mate, our young bobby came straight back down the Roman road from t'other end, like, and ran right into that there scoundrel as he was making his way back to his tent with Baker's hens. I reckon he was caught red-handed in the act, just as he was warned he might be.' He remembered the warning given to him. 'Mind ye,' he added, 'it's only what I reckon.'

'Aye,' put in another. 'Oi did hear tell as Baker had five hens missing. Baker thought it might be the fox.'

'Oh, ah, it were a fox alright, a human fox.'

'And if that there copper ran into him he'd 'rrest him on sight, so to speak, by the light of his lantern,' exclaimed Alvechurch Charlie.

'And there'd be a bit of an 'owdy-do 'atwixt 'em, and if the bobby peeler were having trouble with that slippery customer he'd a-hit him one on the brain-box with his staff, Oi'll bet ye a fiver!'

'Yo ent got no fiver to bet with, Johnny.' The staker was popularly known as Johnny Always Drunk, and it was the truth of this description that made it clear he possessed no means to make a wager.

'Well, there were'nt no handcuffs on that ole scapegoat when they found him in his bed, were there? Now why dint that copper put no handcuffs on him?'

'Oi reckon as how he thought ole Aaron were too measly a little chap to pother with 'em.'

'Ah, and there were a good walk in front of 'em to get to the lock-up in Redditch. Reckon the copper'd think he'd get that little feller there quicker without handcuffs.'

'Aaah. And arter all it warn't a mudder he were taking him in fer, were it? It were only five hens.'

'And when it were mudder he couldna do nought about it because he hadna put them handcuffs on him.' Alvechurch Charlie had it worked out. 'Be gor! Oi'd a put 'em on him.'

'Oh, ah, but you be a measley little chap yeself, bent ye? Ye'd have to to preserve yeself.'

'And he were a wild bird, were Aaron, he wouldna fancy being caged,' put in the landlord, forgetting his duty again.

'Aaaah. And that's where his artfulness came in, fer he musta turned quick like on that bobby and used his knife afore the young feller had time to think.'

'Aaaaah. I reckon it was the idea of being caged as made Aaron go fer him. He woudna stop to think of the consequenshies.'

'Any road up,' the landlord, remembering his duty, gave his summing up of the case: 'there's only one can tell 'xactly what happened along that lane. He wunt tell fer that'd be the death on him if it were him wot dunnit. And t'other can't tell 'cos it be the death on him aready.' These wise considerations, he felt, would cover his former indiscretions.

There were two there listening to the talk who did not join in. The mental picture of a body in a dark lane was still before their minds and exercising such a sense of continued shock that Billy Six-Foot and Tom Branch did not speak unless directly appealed to. In any case they had also be warned against discussing the matter.

The company there, after hearing the tale of the discovery of the body and the subsequent warnings, regarded both men with something like awe and respected their requests to "leave us be".

Aaron Crabtree was committed to the next assizes, for evidence of new findings was sufficient for a charge to be made.

A plaster of Paris cast was made of a certain footprint found near the fowl-pen where five hens had disappeared and which, like the frail, had never been found. This print waas compared with those discovered, not only in the lane where the apparent struggle took place, but also around the poacher's tent.

His boots had gone with the rest of the clothing for examination. On one of the boots was a peculiar bulge caused by a bad repair, and this mark corresponded exactly with a mark on the prints found round the tent, in the lane and near the fowl-pen.

The final macabre discovery was made only a few weeks before the poacher was due to be executed for the murder.

One warm, sunny afternoon in May, Ivy took the three children to the meadow to play, and as was usual they wandered on toward the little brook where they loved to wade in the shallow water, or to hang head down over the miniature bridge as they lay full length on the dry gravel and watched the darting minnows below them. They brought away with them, in jars, the frog-spawn which they would henceforth watch daily for the metamorphosis into first tadpoles, then frogs. Spring, this year was already as warm as summer.

As they passed a pool which was drying out earlier than usual, Edmund called out to Ivy to 'come and look!'

She picked up the baby, two year old Madeline, and went to see what object it was that was causing both boys to hold their noses.

There, held fast in the caked mud, was a frail and it was emitting a foul odour.

Ivy left Madeline on the grassy bank and walked over the dried clay with her own nose pegged firmly between her finger and thumb. She saw that it was full to bursting with the decomposing bodies of several hens.

The girl remembered, then, the story of the missing poultry from the farm across the fields. She picked up Madeline, and calling the boys to follow her home, she went to tell her mistress of the find.

Victoria had John go down to the pool and, on opening the frail, he found the remains of five dead hens, blown up with water, bloated and stinking.

'Urrrgh!' shuddered Ivy. 'That man must have gone straight past Beauchamps that night! I might have come to work and found you all murdered in your beds!'

'Not likely,' rejoined Victoria the sensible, 'it was not we who were trying to arrest him for stealing hens.'

To the dismay of the clergy, Aaron Crabtree was due to pay the ultimate penalty on Whit Monday. It was no so much that they felt any pity since the fellow was receiving his just reward for a felonious deed, but they thought it sacrilegious to hang a felon on the spring holiday which, at that time, was a joyous festival of Christianity.

John thought it ironic. 'After all,' was his caustic comment, 'what's the fuss about? The authorities put to death the man who was too good for this world, and a couple of thieves besides, at the first Easter fesival.'

The clergy organised a petition by which they attempted to persuade "Authority" to postpone the State murder to a more suitable date, but it was unsuccessful.

Aaron ate well and slept well right to the last. He received the ministrations of the church with respect, but he admitted no guilt. In fact he made no statement of any kind and he walked with firm step and head erect to the place of justice, based on a primitive precept three thousand years old, demanding an "eye for an eye" and life for a life.

The last gruseome preparations left him unmoved; amd he died with a brave front that astonished the clergy and left not a few wondering whether a guilty man could behave with such control and dignity.

Conversation at "The Fox and Hounds" consisted of a general summing up by a board of unofficial and unauthorised judges.

'Oh, ah, he got his deserts, did ole Aaron,' was Alvechurch Charlie's opinion. 'But look ye, what a crime to be topped for! Five dead birds what'd fetch less than thirty pieces o' siller in the market.'

'E had a good standing though, did the man, in the face of a bad death, like,' commented Johnny Always Drunk.

'Aaah. It makes ye wonder, don't it? D'ye think, landlord, ther'd be any possibility the chap might be hinnicent?'

'Not him. They do say, them as knows these matters,' answered the landlord, anxious to air his little bit of extra knowlege, 'that a hinnocent man will shout his top off right up to the last moment when he's still got a mouth to shout with, but a guilty un takes it quiet like. He knows he's getting his just deserts, ye see, and I reckon that gives him a sort of satisfaction that right's right in the end. That's what I reckon, mind ye, I wouldn't know for sartin.' The landlord had taken to the habit, lately, of qualifying his remarks by making it clear it was his humble opinion, not dogmatic fact.

'Aaah. But wot a nasty 'ow-d'e do a hanging be. Oi hopes as how it never comes to my lot. Oi'd rather die in me bed wotever sickness it be wot brings me there,' Billy Six-Foot put in.

The vivid picture of the dead body of the poacher after the hanging, painted in telling words by his workmates in the pub, had been superimposed on the mental image of the dead policeman that had been haunting his memory, and this had released him from the first horror by providing a second which he had not actually seen with his own eyes.

'Aye,' answered the landlord, 'but lookye, there was a widder left with three childer on her hands and no breadwinner to keep them from the poor-house or parish relief.'

'Oh, ah, but look at the goodly sum that were collected for 'em.'

'Aaah. A police widder's better off nor wot any of our widders ud be if us went dead on 'em. Who'd give our widders a year's pay and a fine collection of ready money, eh?'

The day after this tribunal gave its findings in "The Fox and Hounds", John met Billy Six-Foot in the Roman lane and, at the point where the policeman met his death, together they set up a memorial by the roadside, with the date of the crime and the initials of the dead constable carved painstakingly on its wooden fence. It stood there for a hundred years commemorating two strange facts: that of a man who lived well and died badly by the hand of a man who lived badly but died well.

This should have been the end of it for Beauchamps, but it was not; for when a disaster occurs or a foul deed is done, those who seem like ghouls come like a flock of vultures descending on their dead prey.

It started way back on a March morning, after the news had first been reported in the newspapers.

Victoria Yeoman chanced to glance through the kitchen window which faced down the long parkland. She noticed that strangers were approaching from the direction of Rowney Green, walking towards the farm by the path she used when she went to the chapel "up the hill".

They walked past the lawn palings and round by the horse pool - so that it was in her mind they must be coming round to the back for eggs or milk, as many did, though usually earlier or later in the day than this. These never arrived. They simply disappeared.

She concluded they must be visitors using the farm track down to Lodge Cottage where an old couple lived by the side of the Roman Lane until, in the afternoon, the same thing happened with another group approaching from the gateway at the end of the rough cart-track leading to the road to Alvechurch. They came up the slope toward the farm — and again they disappeared.

'They must be going down to the Roman lane, Victoria remarked to John. 'Do you think it's plain clothes police, detectives, reporters or what?'

'Can't be,' answered John, 'They all use the official road round.'

'It's sight-seers, Oi'll bet ye,' guessed Ivy.

'Oh, ah, I reckon that's it,' replied John. 'People like a bit of excitement, they get so little of it round here.'

'But there's nothing there now,' objected Ivy.

'Ah, but there is. There's their imaginations.'

'Urrrgh!' shuddered Ivy, 'they wouldn't like it if it happened to someone in their own family.'

'No,' replied John, 'But it hasn't, so they do.'

The following day the same thing happened again. Every day for weeks travellers came past the farm not only on foot, but in dog-carts, in gigs, in wagonettes, carts of all sizes and shapes, even in four horse brakes.

Roger Comptney stood at his window one Sunday and watched them go by. He made his own judgement but he spoke of it to no one except his companion at the window, the landlord of Beauchamps, Charles Bennet.

'They don't really know what they are doing,' he said musingly, 'They don't realise that within each of them they have the same passionate violence as that unfortunate poacher, though it is hidden so deep as to be unrecognised. So we must all have a scape-goat, God forgive us. Innocent or guilty, it does not seem to matter, as long as there is someone to bear the punishment of our hidden guilt.'

Charles Bennet looked at him thoughtfully.

'I hadn't thought of it like that,' he said, 'I suppose there are always those who must go and see the place where, but for the grace of God, they might themselves be, either as victim or killer.'

'Yes, that's it,' agreed Roger. 'Just as the killer feels the urge to revisit the scene of his crime, so these folks are irresistibly drawn to gaze upon the spot where their own inner disasters have been portrayed; their own deepest aggressions are fully realised for them by the savage act of another. That insignificant little old man, though he did not know it, died not only for his own act, but for their secret thoughts as well.'

'Perhaps,' Bennet mused, 'that was the reason, though he could not possibly have realised it, for that strange and unexpected dignity in his bearing when he went to his death.'

THE END

Appendix

INTRODUCTION

Seechem Manor (SP 005217275) lies 1½ miles due east of the centre of Alvechurch, a medieval new town founded and fostered by the lords of the manor, the Bishops of Worcester.

The house is remarkable for a number of reasons. It is a well preserved example of a medieval hall house adapted to 17th and 18th century living requirements. It retains one of the best collections of internal fittings of any farmhouse in the area. They include panelling, a staircase, doors and door furniture, as well as the consolidated remains of a bacon curing chamber. In the surviving cross wing, one of two that once existed here, the panelled first floor room is notable by any standards. The early 19th century alterations, especially the addition of a Gothic porch, are of high quality and are associated with a Birmingham industrialist's plans for a country retreat.

Our understanding of the building is greatly enhanced by the excellent documentary evidence. Local record offices in Worcester, Warwick, Gloucester, Birmingham and Stratford have yielded a rich harvest of manuscript material, whilst national sources in the Public Record Offices have proved especially illuminating for the Civil War period when the house came to prominence as the home of the Parliamentarian, Captain Thomas Milward.

This history is presented as an interim statement of our findings and conclusions so far. A full architectural and historical description will follow, setting out the evidence for the statements and interpretation contained herein.

We are greatly indebted to the owners, Brian and Margery Hearne, and their family, for so much help and encouragement over the past two years enabling us to discover Seechem's history.

HISTORY

The name Seechem was first used in the early 19th century and replaced the building's earlier name of Rowney Green House. This change of name was caused by the building of a new farm, which was carved out of the western side of the original estate, and became Rowney Green Farm. The modern hilltop settlement of Rowney Green was, until the early 1800s, wasteland around the edge of which a number of cottages had been built. It was then known as Great Rowney Green to distinguish it from unenclosed land lying to the north and east of Seechem, known as Little Rowney Green.

The survival of the core of a hall house proves that the site was occupied during the medieval period. This consists of a two bay open hall with indications of a cross-passage at the lower end (roof plan, trusses TI-TIV). At the upper end there was a solar cross-wing. The smoke-blackened hall roof had a central open truss with arch-braced cambered tie-beam, raking struts and curved wind braces.

No medieval documentary evidence has yet been found which can be correlated with the surviving open hall. The medieval hamlets of Pyrley and Febley lay a little to the north-west and east of this site respectively, but neither can be positively associated with this house on present evidence.

In the late 16th century freehold land at Rowney Green came into the possession of the Milward family, who had long been resident in the parish of Alvechurch. At the same time they acquired a moiety of the manor of 'Green', which they shared with the Actons of Longfield Manor and the Moores of Moor Green Hall. The manor of Green, which lay within the Bishop of Worcester's manor of Alvechurch, may be equated with the manorial estate centred on the medieval moated site lying at the foot of Weatheroak Hill.

In the 1580s Thomas Milward sold his Rowney Green estate to his uncle William Milward, a prominent citizen and haberdasher of London, who was also a member of the Merchant Adventurers, the leading overseas trading company. When William died in London in 1582 he made provision for his Alvechurch lands to pass to the eldest male heir or to younger sons, so that they shall 'remayne in the name of the Milwards for ever.' Until 1592 the Milward's house at Rowney Green had been let to Thomas Knight, but Thomas Milward, as chief beneficiary of his father's estate, now moved in. A gentleman farmer, known locally as 'Lusty Milward,' he used his inherited wealth to improve his Alvechurch estate and served as Bailiff of the Bishop of Worcester's Manor of Alvechurch for many years.

Thomas was presumably responsible for the extensive alterations to the house at this time. These included the building of a new parlour cross-wing on the site of the solar, the insertion of floors and a chimney into the open hall and the creation of a lobby entrance against the stack. The new cross-wing was of at least five bays, four of which survive (roof plan, tursses T1-T5). The framing, which has recently been exposed, is close studded to the ground floor and three square panels high above. In the West Midlands this pattern may be dated to the period c 1590-1610 and is found locally at Scarfield Farm, which is dated by documentary evidence to 1601-2.

The parlour cross-wing, rebuilt about 1600, was remodelled about 20 or 30 years later. First floor windows were inserted in the side wall frame and an external staircase was built. A chimney stack was added to the northernmost bay, which heated the parlour and the chamber over it. In addition the first floor chamber, now known as the Oak Room or Great Chamber was fully panelled. A carved ornamental of three arcaded bays divided by Doric columns surrounds and surmounts the stonework of the fireplace. Draughts from the landing and door to the outside staircase were shielded by an internal porch, whereby the panelling protruded into the room as a small square lobby or 'portal door'. This has since been reset against the walls but its original position may still be seen in the floor boards and in the plaster ceiling.

No less than 23 rooms are listed in the inventory. Even allowing for the sub-division of once larger rooms, hinted at by descriptions like 'the Little Chamber within the parlour', and the fact that the parlour cross-wing extended further to the south-east, it is clear that the house was then considerably larger. Fortunately the estate map of 1701 depicts a bird's eye view of Seechem and shows a cross-wing at the south-west end of the hall range, its site now occupied by the 19th century dairy.

This large and comfortable timber-framed house passed in 1638 to the eldest son, also called Thomas Milward, who was then 21 years old and had only recently matriculated from Trinity College, Oxford. Thomas pursued a legal career becoming a barrister at Lincoln's Inn, so that his home life on the eve of the Civil War was split between London and Alvechurch.

Thomas Milward's sympathies lay with Parliament; in September 1644 he became a member of the influential County Committee and in the following month was appointed captain of a troop of horse within Colonel Thomas Archer's regiment. Very detailed accounts survive for the management of his troop, showing Captain Milward collecting taxes to pay some 124 officers and soldiers, including his brother Clement as Lieutenant. We see Milward moving his troop around the Midlands, quartering his men and horses in Warwick in June 1664 and August 1645, marching into south Warwickshire taking part in the siege of Worcester in 1646. On a local level we see Thomas Milward's troop harassing Royalists, snatching horses from the Earl of Shrewsbury, stables at Grafton Manor and from the Middlemore's at Hawkesley House, King's Norton. Milward's neighbours looked on in awe as he rose to prominence. Ralph Bell testified in 1705 that 'between 50 and 60 years ago Captain Thomas Milward ...Justice of the Peace and a grate man in Oliver's day... that when he enclosed part of Little Rowney Green and built 'a great barn' on part of it 'the inhabitants durst not oppose him.'

At the Restoration Milward obtained a royal pardon the General Monck, having travelled to Breda with Sir Thomas Clarges as part of the delegation to invite Charles Stuart to return to England. However, arrears of pay, due not only to himself but to his soldiers, the expenses of which he had borne, caused Milward financial hardship forcing him to sell the Alvechurch estate in 1663. The estate, centred round Rowney Green House, included 200 acres of farmland, stretched from Icknield Street on the east to the edge of the Bishop's Park bounded by Rowney Green Lane on the west as well as three other houses and a cottage. In addition Thomas Milward owned, but let, the Bear Inn (now the House) on Bear Hill in Alvechurch, which may have been owned by the family earlier in the 17th century.

Henceforward until the end of the 19th century the house was let to tenant farmers. The purchaser of the Milward estate, Richard Booth, was a London grocer who let the house to branches of the Parsonage family from the late 1680s. This involved a certain amount of replanning and rebuilding, the latter attested by the repositioned date stone '1668' in the kitchen. These alterations included the enlargement of the back to back fireplace in the former open hall, kitchen proportions to enable the house to be split between two households. A bacon curing chamber was installed on the first floor level in the same stack. Its remains were uncovered and consolidated in 1986. They consist of two smoke blackened and salt-ridden walls with a tall narrow door opening into the main chimney and a small return flue above.

A list of 18th century tenant farmers has been compiled from leases, landtax records and maps. They include... tenant farmers: Edward Smith from 1765 to 1772, George and later Sarah Birch c 1788 and finally John Avery between 1792 and 1817. In that year John Moore offered his Rowney Green estate for auction. It was purchased by James Luckcock (1761-1835), the Birmingham buckle and button manufacturer. Luckcock intended to take up residence at Seechem, a lodge was built at the end of the drive near Icknield Street changing the main access from the north to the east side of the house, where a single storeyed porch in Gothic style was added to the parlour cross-wing.

The frame of this cross-wing, which appears to have been painted black and white in the late 18th century, was now rendered with stucco and scored to represent ashlar. Luckcock's brother had experimented with fanciful architecture when he built himself a thatched and stuccoed folly to live in, now the Round House in St James's Road, Edgbaston. Despite the building work at Seechem which included the building of a dairy on the site of the west cross-wing, James Luckcock stayed in Birmingham, preferring to build himself a new house in George Road, Edgbaston. Seechem was accordingly let, firstly to John Holbeach until his death in 1862 and secondly from then until c 1873 to his son Jonathan. Thomas Godwin was farming there as a tenant of the Beale family in 1876 and was succeeded in 1879 by George Quinney. The Quinney family bought the farm sometime afterwards and farmed it themselves until its sale to the present owners in 1983.